# How to Keep Going

(with your book, business or creative project)

# When You Want to Give Up

Practical inspiration to help you create good habits
and stay focused – even when it's hard

## Robbie Swale

Winds of Trust Publications

ISBN 978-1-915266-01-9

# Contents

## Part Three: NEGOTIATE THE ONLINE COMPARISON TRAPS

## Part Four: DON'T LOSE HEART – LESSONS FOR THE DARK DAYS

'*The willingness to show up changes us. It makes us a little braver each time.*'

–Brené Brown

# Impact

'I was paralysed by fear and indecision until I came across Robbie's work. Now, thanks to the 12-Minute Method, I believe that I am an author and I am writing my first book.'
**Nadine Kelly, M.D.,**
**Founder of NPK Health Integration**


'"Surely I can find 12 minutes in a day," I thought when I saw Robbie's workshop on "how to write a book in 12 minutes". It was a low barrier to entry towards creating a sustainable writing practice. It was the best decision I have made. I have now published a book and have been writing for 483 consecutive days. I would not have done that had it not been for Robbie's idea, but more importantly seeing him walk his talk with the 12-Minute Method.'
**Karena de Souza**
**Author, Contours of Courageous Parenting**


'Robbie's writing and 12-Minute Method inspired me to finally take the first steps to start a business I'd had in my mind (and done nothing about) for years. Learning to lean into resistance and just take the first step has had a huge impact on my mindset, mental health, family and career development. In the four years since, we have become a successful, award-winning business! I'm extremely grateful to Robbie for his genuinely impactful and thought provoking 12-minute articles.'

**Paul Thompson**

**Founder/Health and Wellbeing Coach and Consultant, WorkSmart Wellbeing**


'I wouldn't have written any of what I have without Robbie's example and his 12-minute approach. It's what gave me the initial courage to try such a writing practice myself, to break through both fear and creative blockage… and then to post one article, then several, and then to become known for such writing. When someone mentioned I should write a book, the only thing that gave me the confidence to believe I could, was seeing what Robbie had already accomplished. I am on page 316 of my flash draft.'

**Peter Tavernise**

**Leadership Coach**


'As a true believer in the power of creativity to fire us up and get us into action, I see Robbie as a real leader in the field. His ability to excite and inspire even the most reluctant participants is really impressive. Whether in academia, tech, finance, culture or anything in between, Robbie will help you put aside the noise and focus on what is really important to you.'

**Jo Hunter**

**Co-Founder and CEO, 64 Million Artists**

'The ethos of the 12-Minute Method is inspiring and challenging, but it is hearing what led Robbie to it in the first place that connects most. Words matter, but so does the spirit and story behind the words, and that's what catches me more than anything about Robbie's writing.'

**Dr Hannah Mather**
**Executive Coach, Theologian, and Author, The Interpreting Spirit**


'Many times, in many ways, I have recommended the 12-Minute Method to others and watched them come alive with inspiration when they hear how Robbie brought this book to life. His genius ideas are exponentially valuable. To me, it's the 12-Minute Miracle.'

**Michelle C. Basey**
**Energy Healing Artist and CoreYou Coach**


'Robbie will get an acknowledgment in my second book, as he did in my first. The second couldn't have been written without the first and the first would never have been written without Robbie's leadership and his 12-Minute Method. His fingerprints are forever more on anything I publish! Robbie's guidance will support your progress and lead you to share the 12-Minute Method with others. It's that good.'

**David W. Reynolds**
**Creator and host of the Lead. Learn. Change. Podcast; Author, Lead. Learn. Change**

'I would highly recommend Robbie to anyone who is facing what feels like an insurmountable hurdle, whether it's personal or professional.'

**Emma Kerr**
**Senior Global Practice Specialist, DAI**

'I've always liked to write, however, I'm not a writer. Why would I write, if I'm not a writer? Stumbling upon Robbie's 12-Minute Method gave me permission to write. Anyone can be a writer for 12 minutes! Since incorporating the method into my weekly routine, and publishing on social, I am considered by many to be a "thought leader" in my space.'

**Bryon Howard**
**CEO, The Howard Team Real Estate Services – eXp Realty**

'Each time I talk with Robbie, he gives me a new thought to think about.'

**Robert Holden**
**Author, Authentic Success**

'Whatever progress you wish you could make in your career, or more generally in your life – whether it's starting a business, writing your first book, or any other new beginning – Robbie's 12-Minute Method will help you overcome the obstacles in your way, focus your energy and start!'

**Alex Swallow**
**Author, How To Become An Influencer**

# About The Author

*Written on 13th October 2021*

I'm Robbie Swale, a writer and coach.

There have been many times in my life where I didn't get my ideas off the ground, where I was stuck in creative hell and where I wasn't productive. Thankfully, mostly that has changed.

Now people call me prolific and that's all down to the lessons I learned while creating the 12-Minute Method. Some of the things I have beaten procrastination to do and finally got off the ground include:

- A blog, clocking in at over 200 articles; each written in 12 minutes

- A coaching business, built from nothing, that could support me full-time in less than two years

- *Aprendiendo español* (I've got a long way to go, but I'm moving and not stopping)

- A website dedicated to my favourite author, now containing over 300 inspirational snippets of wisdom (read more at **www.wisdomofgemmell.com**)

- A podcast, including interviews with best-selling authors and world-famous coaches (**www.thecoachsjourney.com**)

- Books: two out now, including this one, two more due in 2022, and another that's almost finished
- A career change
- Getting married

I spent the first decade of my career doing lots of different things. I was a director, a trustee, a manager, almost a professional actor, a leader and an administrator.

In my current work, I'm interested in three things:

*Creativity* (and why people don't do the things they want to do).

*Leadership* and how people can be honourable in their work. How they can find success without feeling like they have to compromise their values and identity.

*Coaching*: the amazing craft that allows each of us to develop vital skills for our future and to more often be our wisest and most skilful selves.

I've coached people working on amazing creative ideas, from businesses to books and beyond. I've worked with people on many incredible projects that you will never have heard of. I've also worked, coached, trained and facilitated for organisations like Swiss Re, the University of Edinburgh, the Royal Opera House, Moonpig, UCL and more.

I'm proud to be an associate of 64 Million Artists, an organisation dedicated to unleashing the creativity of everyone in the UK, and a Fellow Coach for BetterUp, the world's biggest mental health and coaching organisation.

Mostly, though, I'm proud that I've felt fear, felt resistance, felt the pull of procrastination, and I've battled it, knowing that that battle was a battle for my soul: to take me out of creative hell and grow me into someone new. There have been many ideas that haven't made it because I didn't know how to fight that battle. But my line is drawn: *not anymore.*

Read more about me and sign up to my mailing list at:

**www.robbieswale.com**

# About This Book

This is a book about how to keep going. How to not give up.

It's not a 'how to' book in the traditional sense. Well, it is. Here's the 'how to':

*Choose your habit. Stick with it. Don't give up.*

Simple. But not easy.

The rest of the book is about inspiration and ideas. It's about giving YOU what YOU need to fulfil that simple but often incredibly difficult thing: to keep going when (on some level) you want to give up.

That level isn't always in our conscious mind. Often, we say we *want* to do something, and we don't *intend* to give up. But if we find ourselves slipping in our habits and not meeting our commitments, then the truth is, on some level, that some part of us has chosen to do something other than 'that thing' we thought we wanted to do.

That's complex. People are complex. So is the creative process. So are the reasons some of us don't do the things we want to do; that we give up even when we say we don't want to.

That's why this isn't (apart from the few sentences above) a 'how to' book in the traditional sense.

Instead, in this book you'll find ideas and practical inspiration to help you become someone who keeps going, who doesn't give up. When you can become that person – as I've found through my creative battles and my 12-minute writing practice – then *everything* changes.

When you can truly believe that you are the person who won't give up, then everything you want is only a matter of time away. Nothing feels impossible; everything feels like something you can choose.

That's how important this is.

So read this book looking for the inspiration that will help you; the stuff that will help you during those moments where you might previously have given up.

Look for the keys that will help you to develop resilience, courage, and bloody-mindedness in the face of your struggles and fear.

You'll find sections on resisting distractions and maintaining focus, on dealing with yourself, on the challenges of comparison in the internet age, and on what to do on the dark days, in the really difficult times.

Read for insight. Sometimes we only need one idea to change things for us. Set your intention now to find that idea, whichever one it is for you, as you read this book.

If you want help with that, I've created a worksheet to record your insights as you go. For some of us it's very easy to 'just read' a book and not put the ideas it contains into action. If that's you, download the worksheet here:

**www.robbieswale.com/12minute-method-downloads**

This book has been created to be read in order, so you can read it like that. But the most important thing about the way you read this book is that you engage with it in a way that allows you to become a person who doesn't give up. So, do what you need to do to become that person.

That might mean reading it from start to finish. It might mean skipping about liberally. For you, it might be dipping in on the days when you need help with something in particular. Or it might be scanning the chapter headings for whatever catches your eye today, and trusting that that chapter will contain what you need to help you keep going; to help you not give up.

Not every chapter or idea in this book will be right for you. But there will be some that are. There will be some, collected by me over years of struggling with keeping going, struggling with creativity, that will make a difference.

And never forget that sometimes one idea is all we need.

So, make this book work for you. Don't worry about any

of the conventions, just use it to keep going. To not give up. To become someone who can keep their promises to themselves. Who can hold their commitments.

And, through that, use it to be someone who follows through on their ideas, who makes work that counts.

Use it to get *that* idea out of you and into the world. You know the one. The one that's calling you. The one you wish you'd done already.

That's what matters.

*Robbie Swale*

*11th March, 2022*

# The 12-Minute Method

The 12-Minute Method emerged from my struggles. It emerged from a feeling of anxiety and stress every time I thought about sharing something online. Even trivial things – putting a joke I had thought of on Facebook – became an event in my life, and not a pleasant one. One full of tension and worry. One usually ending with me *not* posting something online even though I'd planned to.

I was in the middle of a rich period of discovery in my life. I was changing career, setting out on a new way of working, and was finally truly open to the fact that I could change my experience of life by changing how I thought and who I was. I was working with a coach, Joel Monk, and I took my struggles with sharing things to those sessions. Those sessions with Joel were so rich, and one of the richest moments came when we designed a practice.

I had realised that there was something special about my short train journey from Clapham Junction to Waterloo. I'll tell you more about that later, in the chapter We're Already Moving. There was a freedom in this time, and we began to talk about creating a writing practice. It wasn't the first writing I'd published online, but it was the writing that was going to change me forever.

One of the most magical moments was when Joel shared that in his previous life as a visual artist, he had liked to create series of paintings. What if I created a series of articles? And so, we designed it: the train series. It was due to be written on that train journey, once a day, on each of the days I was taking the train to London in the next two weeks. That was five times, it turned out. Here was the practice:

Get on the train. Start writing. Write while the train is moving. Stop when the train stops. Proofread it once, then post it online.

I decided to post the articles on LinkedIn because… well… I thought no one read LinkedIn! But it turned out they did. People 'liked' the articles. Not many, but a few. And some even commented.

And perhaps most importantly for my fears, no one hated them. Or at least they didn't say they did. I didn't die. I wasn't humiliated. Those reactions sound melodramatic, but that's how intense the fear was. Really.

After writing those five articles I went on holiday. And over the holiday I reflected. I noticed there was something about this writing, this practice, that felt important and valuable. So, I decided to make it into a longer commitment. It would become a weekly practice. One article a week, written on my train journey. More than that would have been too many. Less than that would have been too few. One a week felt about right.

And, for the purposes of this book, a book about sticking with things, not giving up, about keeping your promise to yourself week after week, that was a key moment. I didn't quit my practice after the five articles. And I designed a practice after that, one which I could keep going with. A key moment.

And it was followed by a series of key moments, one every week, when I decided not to give up, when I decided to keep going. When I didn't quit.

After a little while, I stopped getting the train as regularly, but the practice was already important to me by then, so I needed to think about how to continue it when I wasn't on the train. I checked how long the train journey took the next time I got it. It took 12 minutes. And there we have it, the 12-Minute Method:

Sit.

Set a timer for 12 minutes.

Write while the timer is going, stop when the timer stops.

Proofread it once, then post it online.

That's part of the 12-Minute Method, anyway.

It was about three years later when I discovered the depth of the 12-Minute Method that I had accidentally uncovered.

Inspired by marketing guru Seth Godin releasing a book compiling several years of his blog, I thought, 'I could make *my* blog posts into a book.' I had been writing for three years, once a week, meaning there were about 150 articles. And because they were all posted on LinkedIn, I realised that if there was someone who liked the articles, they would find it hard to actually read them. Putting them all in one place would be helpful to the people – no matter how few there might be – who wanted to read my writing. Not doing that was really only hurting them and me, and it wasn't helping anyone. Plus, I thought, I could call it something funny like *I Wrote This Book in 12 Minutes*.

As I was thinking about how to do this, I talked to my friend Steve, a copy editor who I was hoping to enlist to help me turn 150-odd blog posts into a book. He said, 'That's a great title,' then asked an interesting question: *Can the book itself do what the title does?* Can it be an inspiration to get out of your own way and create something, just like you, Robbie, created this book?

And it turned out that it could. I sat down with three years of blog posts, printed them all off and spread them out across our living room. I thought, if this is a book to stop people procrastinating and get them creating something, what might the stages look like? And as I looked through those pieces, it turned out that I had been writing very much about what it takes to create something from nothing; about the act of creativity, of entrepreneurialism, of changing things for the better.

Really, this shouldn't have surprised me, but of course it did.

It shouldn't have surprised me because I had been writing for three years in an emergent way. There's not much time to plan a piece when you're writing to a 12-minute timer.

It's about what's in the front of your mind. What are you interested in today? What do you have something to say about this week?

What I had been interested in and what was at the front of my mind during those three years was fighting my creative battles. Getting through my procrastination. Stopping being someone that ideas and opportunities passed by and becoming someone who made things happen.

Not only that, but I had been working as a coach, helping people make the changes in their lives that mattered most, whether in their career, as a leader, as a creator, or in their relationships. So, I had become more and more familiar with the stages that are required to make a change, and the ways in which people struggle.

So, writing in an emergent way over those three years, and seeing what emerged each time I sat down, had rather unsurprisingly (and surprisingly) become a story about how humans struggle with making change happen and what can help us to counteract those struggles.

I had, in fact, written a book about something. About the things I had been most interested in. About how we beat procrastination, become more productive, and finally do those things that we desperately, deep down, want to do.

And in that book, four stages emerged.

First, we have to start. Nothing we want to create can exist unless we start it. Everything that exists was started at some point. It can be the hardest part of the journey, the first step, and we might think of it as the most important, the most fundamental. That, of course, is the subject of my first book, *How to Start When You're Stuck*.

Next, we have to keep going. In some ways, this is the hardest stage. If starting is hard, keeping going is like that but repeated. Keeping going is, really, just starting again every day or week. Resisting the inertia that pulls us back to the place where we are still and not moving. The practice of keeping going is vital, and that's what this book is here to help you with.

The third part of the creative process, if we want to do our best work, is to create the conditions for great work to happen. We can't control creativity, it's too complex for that. But we can make ourselves more prone to accidentally creating something magical. That's what the first two parts of the process do: *starting* and *keeping going* make it infinitely more likely that we will do some great work, as opposed to not starting, or starting then soon giving up. But there's more we can do. We can create habits, relationships, ways of thinking and more, which will make us that little bit more likely to strike the magical place where our unique talents and the chance of creativity collide to make something that truly matters, to us or to others.

Finally, if we want to give our work the chance to change more than just us, we have to *share* it. If we want our work to really count, we have to get it out into the world. And, as the origin of my writing practice shows, that can be the hardest part. But it matters. At least, I believe it does. Because I believe that ordinary people like you and me making work that matters is what will change the world. So we *have* to share our work.

So the 12-Minute Method has two levels. On one level, it is the power of a short, regular practice, undertaken every week. On another level, it is this four-stage process:

1. Start.
2. Keep going.
3. Create the conditions for great work.
4. Share it.

And this order matters. It may sound obvious, but the first two things to give your attention to are the first two things in that list. Can you start? Can you keep going? I want to repeat myself: nothing in the creative process is more important than these two things.

I have seen many creative projects – mine and many other people's – wrecked on the rocks of 'creating the perfect conditions' before focusing on starting.

*I'll start my business when I have my home office set up.*

*I'll start my book when I know for sure what I want my book to be about.*

*I'll start my new project when my work has calmed down and I can find the headspace to write.*

They sound like legitimate reasons, but they are all procrastination and Resistance. Ways in which our brains endeavour to keep us 'safe', but actually prevent us from growing into someone new.

It's important to say that, yes, it does matter that you create the conditions for great work, but the most important condition for great work is that you are working. That you start and you keep going, every day or week, practising what you practise, getting better, becoming someone whose resilience allows them to keep going.

And that *keeping going* is the subject of this book. Starting matters, but the thing that has really changed me has been seeing that I am someone who can keep going and keep going and keep going. I am someone who can commit to something and see it through.

Through this process I have seen that it is by habits that we change. In 12 minutes a week I have become, over what is now five and a half years, and more than 200 articles, someone who writes. Not just that, but like the tortoise and the hare, my slow persistence makes me now one of the most prolific writers I know. People who had written 20, 30, even 100 articles before I had written one, have now written fewer than me.

And I've seen that through building these habits, suddenly time is on my side. Before starting, I was full of regret. Why didn't I start two years ago? Then suddenly, two more years had gone by and the regret had doubled: why didn't I start *four* years ago? But now, with each passing month, a new set of four or five articles by me appears online. With each month I am more prolific. And that is available to you, too.

Setting a habit, setting a practice, even for just 12-minutes a week, to work on your book or your business or your creative project, will show you, over time, something that I really should have known all along but didn't:

**If you start something, and do even a little bit every week, over years you will create something. You will change and – if you stick with it, if you don't give up – you might create something magical.**

I created this book and the others in the series (in the end I decided that for people to get the most from this writing, it would work better as a series, one book about each stage). I didn't mean to, I just showed up and didn't stop showing up. Then I looked at what I'd made. More than 80,000 words in three years. Almost without noticing. All, really, because I didn't quit.

Because when I felt like quitting, or when I missed a week (as you'll hear in this book, that did happen) I recommitted. I made sure I managed myself, so that I kept going through the dark days. I held focus in all the ways I could. I wrestled with the online comparison traps and survived. And I kept my habit going.

One week at a time.

That's what I want for you. I want it so that you will change, so that you will become someone who doesn't give up. Whose graft and courage resist the pulls of procrastination and distraction. Whose commitment to their art – whether it is a business, a book, or something else – matters enough for them to grow as a human. Whose desire to be someone new outweighs the fears and struggles you (and those around you) have that conspire to keep you the same.

I want this because I think that the work you will do matters. And the work that really matters can't be done in one sitting. It needs to be done by someone who sits down repeatedly, mastering their craft, practising and not giving up, making something, and making something, and making something else.

Over and over again we have to practise if we want to discover our unique genius. If we want to be the most we can be.

Over and over again we have to start.

I can tell you this: it does get easier. It's not always as hard as the first start. And once we've seen this in one area of our life, we can take it to another. When we have become someone who can make a commitment to ourselves and keep it, then that will never leave us. And that is one of the most powerful capabilities we can develop in ourselves. Are you someone who keeps your promises to yourself?

I wasn't. Not always. But I am now.

That's why we need to practise being honest with ourselves. That's why we need to practise not giving up.

That's what I hope this book helps you with. I hope it helps you choose something to keep going with and then keep going, taking inspiration from my struggles and the ideas shared in the following pages.

I care about releasing the creative potential of people like you, because I believe there's a magical idea in you. A business that will change people's lives, a book that will change how people feel or think. Or simply a change in you that will, through leadership and all your relationships, inspire and change the world around you. Something that is calling you.

And once you've found that thing, I hope you'll keep practising, keep going, keep learning and keep changing things. Because that – all of us doing our part – is how we'll change this world together.

Being someone who gives up on things can feel like hell. Seeing what other people, who started at the same time as you, have become when you haven't is a feeling many of us know intimately. The envy, maybe jealousy. The self-criticism. Giving up on ideas, on changes we want to make, is normal. And it's the scourge of positive change.

Persistence, becoming someone who doesn't give up, that changes everything.

We're all on the same ship here. Let's steady it by steadying ourselves. By doing work that matters and by not giving up. By showing up, week after week until the world – even just our corner of it – is better.

Let's start. And keep going. And keep going.
And keep going.

# Free 12-Minute Method Action Sheet

I want you to use this book to keep your idea going, to not give up, to keep working and persisting until your idea is out in the world. So, I've created a worksheet that guides you through creating your own 12-minute practice and gives you somewhere to turn the insights you get from this book into action.

It also includes some recommended further reading from the thinkers and authors who have influenced this book and the rest of the series, whose names you'll find in the chapters that follow.

You can download the action sheet for free at:
**www.robbieswale.com/12minute-method-downloads**
or by scanning this QR code:

# Part One: HOLD YOUR FOCUS AND RESIST DISTRACTIONS

The line between persistence and giving up has always mattered. It has always been the difference between the one-time playwright and Shakespeare. Between the band who played 10 gigs and the Beatles. Between the coffee shops that folded and the high street chains that are more famous than rock stars.

But the modern world has made that line even more stark. In Silicon Valley and elsewhere, some of the smartest people in the world are competing with each other to build AI systems that are as distracting as possible, that hold our attention for as long as possible. Of course, we benefit from those systems. For example, especially during the coronavirus pandemic, the importance of being able to communicate with each other across distance was never more vital to our social lives, our work, our mental health and more.

Yet, as a result of technology and more, there are *so many* distractions, so many ways to procrastinate.

In some ways, the only question we need to answer in order to be persistent, to not give up, is: are we willing to sit down every day or week and do the work? Avoid the distractions and focus on what counts. Again, and again, and again.

Of course, it's not as easy as that. There are myriad reasons to make choices that aren't to sit down every week, and not all of them are bad choices; not all of them feel like the devil on our shoulder, talking us out of what matters.

Yet, if we want to create something, if we want to show up week after week, we have to choose to do that. We have to find the ways to resist distractions, to hold our focus and to stick to our guns.

That's what Part One of this book is about. It contains ideas, practices and reminders that I hope will give you the inspiration you need to resist the calls of the sirens, no matter how pernicious and wonderful those calls might be, and keep going.

Keep going because the work you're doing matters, to you and to others. Keep going because, if you do, you'll make something magical.

# Chapter One

# The Secret to Getting Things Done: Sit Down and Stay Sitting

*Written on 7th August, 2019*

God, it's hard to get things done sometimes. I'm working on a book at the moment. This book has been on each of my Warren Buffet lists of five things to do by dd/mm/yy since I first used that powerful goal-setting exercise in 2017, and I've been working on the book since 2016.[1] I made a deal with myself when I wrote *Publish Possibility Writing* (my working title at the time) on my list for 2019 that it wouldn't be on my list for 2020. But it's *hard*.

The last two days of working on it have been some of the hardest. I've felt stressed, anxious, unable to think. I know this is what happens. I know from all the writers I've ever heard talk about the process that there are bits of it that AREN'T FUN. I know from Steven Pressfield that Resistance gets stronger near the finish line.

But that doesn't make it any less hard. And how do I *know* if this book is actually worth sharing? How do I know if a thought is Resistance, or if I really am wasting energy on a dud project? Is the doubt an accurate picture of me and what I have to say? Or is it just my ego's way of saying,

'Don't grow so much by doing this that I have to die and be replaced by a new sense of self'?

Over the last six months, even while working on this book and my other four priorities for this year, I have been full of ideas. Some have been for me, some for clients, some for fellow participants on Seth Godin's Marketing Seminar. Sitting, feeling incredibly excited about one of them a few weeks ago, I thought, 'Oh wow, even these ideas are Resistance.' Get that… *even my new ideas are Resistance.* And, even if I say so myself, some of them are *great* ideas.

But if I believe in the work Steven Pressfield shared in books like *The War of Art*[2] (and I do) then I have to remember what he says: that the more Resistance we feel towards something, the more important that thing is for our soul's evolution. And boy, do I have a lot of Resistance to working on this book.

I might be wrong about this book. It might be terrible. And by sharing something terrible, my soul will grow.

I might be wrong *in* the book: it might get me into trouble with people who disagree with me. And by getting into that trouble, my soul will grow.

It might be boring and no one will want to read it. And, by publishing and sharing something boring, my soul will grow.

And, of course, I might be wrong about *all* those things: it might be good, it might speak to people, it might be interesting and funny and engaging. And then my soul will grow.

Or it might be somewhere in between. And then my soul will grow.

One of the key ideas in the 'possibility writing' book is that *you can choose* what goes on in your head far more than you think. And despite that, it takes me writing a piece like this to remember that *I can choose* to believe that Pressfield is right. When I choose that, then I keep going with this book. When I choose that, I keep sitting down, no matter how hard it is, no matter how hard it feels. Day after day.

'There's a secret that real writers know that wannabe writers don't,' says Pressfield in *The War of Art*. 'And the secret is this: it's not the writing part that's hard. What's hard is sitting down to write.'

There is certainly something to be said, in the modern world, for flitting around; for being responsive to opportunities and being nimble in our work. But there's also something to be said for commitment. For holding our word to ourselves. For having the force of will to see things through. *To sit down*, even when we don't want to. To do the hard part, even when we don't want to.

As the distractions get bigger and the world moves faster, sitting down and focusing, despite all that, might just be the ability that is most needed. If you have that ability – to see what is most important for you to work on, then to sit down, over and over again, and each time you sit down to *stay sitting* until your time is up – then you will create something.

The publisher Maurice Bassett told me a story about his friend, Colin Wilson, who realised that if you write 1,000 words a day for a year, you end up with 365,000 words. That's three *long* books.

To do that, you have to sit down and stay sitting.

When will you sit down, and what will you do while you are there?

## Notes

1. The book in question is not this one. It's an as-yet-still-unpublished book provisionally titled *The Power to Choose*. You can read a draft of some of the chapters of it on my website here: https://www.robbieswale.com/writing/2020/3/23/why-am-i-sharing-parts-of-my-forthcoming-book-the-power-to-choose. The Warren Buffet exercise in question is what I write about briefly under number 3 in this article: https://www.robbieswale.com/writing/2018/7/23/15-ways-to-change-your-relationship-to-time-get-more-done-and-feel-better-while-you-do-it

2. You'll find references to Steven Pressfield's work and his concept, Resistance, throughout this book. Resistance, which he first wrote about in *The War of Art*, has been one of the most powerful ideas in helping me to win my creative battles. It is his word for all the ways we conspire not to do the things that really matter.

# Chapter Two

# Choose What is Important, Not What Feels Nice

*Written on 6th January, 2017*

Balance is such an important word in today's culture in the UK. Work-life balance is one of the most common things people want to talk about when they speak to me about coaching. I personally try not to use that phrase, dating back to a lesson I learned in the Waking Up the Workplace interview series. It implies, after all, that work isn't life. And that would be a sad state of affairs.

But balance. Balance is key.

In particular, it is important to consider a different balance: between *what feels nice now* and *what we do because it is an important thing for us to do*. This is a hard balance to hold.

Fred Kofman, in his book *Conscious Business*, talks about climbing mountains as an example of this. It isn't fun. It isn't nice. It is painful and frightening and, on some mountains, many people don't make it to the top; don't achieve what they set out to achieve. But when Kofman is doing it, he knows that he will look back on it with pride. It will be a memory he cherishes, for the experience it gives him, and because, well... because it is an important thing for him to do.

Just before Christmas, I let the *feeling nice* part of things get in the way of me writing one of these articles. I was tired and worried about the work I had on that day, and I was stressed about Christmas. I was also a little shaken (in the aftermath of the terrorist attack in Berlin) by all the trains stopping eerily around Clapham Junction railway station after a driver had pulled the emergency cord.

I had been planning to write one final article of 2016, but instead, panicked by my state of affairs, I gave myself a break. For 12 minutes things were nicer. I read my book and relaxed. I didn't write. It was nice. But I also lost out. I lost out artistically. What might I have written in that state? From that particular place of vulnerability, who knows what might have emerged? And I lost out in my commitment to myself: to write an article every week to the end of the year.

It's important to look after yourself. But it's also important to win your creative battles. To beat Resistance. So when you are feeling tired, and you decide not to fulfil the commitment that you know is the right thing for you to do, that you know you will look back on with pride, pleased that it was something you did, remember this.

# Chapter Three

# Sometimes it Doesn't Matter If What You Believe Is True, It Matters If It Is Useful

*Written on 15th January, 2019*

My nerves are more than a little frayed at the moment. I'm in the build-up to running my group programme for coaches – The Coach's Journey – for the second time. In the middle of this process I have time off for Christmas and then another holiday, which I'm going on at the end of the week. Compared to most of my normal business, The Coach's Journey is different, particularly because in order to run it I need several people to say 'Yes' at the same time. That's very different to the way I mostly work with new clients: finding exactly the right time to start our work for both of us, even if that is months or years after we first connect.

One of the effects of this is that I find this period in my year more stressful, and I have some ideas that I remind myself of in the midst of that stress, in the midst of the vulnerability and the accompanying fear that *this might not work* (which I try to remind myself is always present when you are creating something... it has to be there, to go with the potentially joyous other outcome: *this might work*).

One of the most useful things I remind myself of is that, whatever happens with this programme, all the energy I am putting out into the world to market it is having an impact, and will do in the future for my work. The marketing is useful in the long term, whether I sell places on the programme or not. I am forging new connections, reconnecting with people I haven't been in contact with for weeks or months, creating content and sharing it with the world.

I shared this with an old friend of mine at the weekend:

'I'm tired and my nerves are a bit frayed, but I'm putting all this energy out into the world and I know it will come back.'

My friend questioned this, pointing out, 'That doesn't sound scientific, but I kind of get what you mean.'

Now, part of the confusion in this conversation may have been one of language. I do believe that there is a correlation between how often I tell people about my work and connect with new people and how much business I create. But a thought occurred to me:

*Does it matter if this is true?*

I'm currently reading Matthew Syed's fascinating book *Bounce*, about how it is *practice* and not *talent* that is important for excellence and success. Among many wonderful stories from the worlds of sport and psychology and beyond, Syed writes at length about the placebo effect. The stories include fascinating things about the way humans work. How, for instance, different coloured placebo tablets work better for different ailments and this takes us, in the end, to a thought like the one that occurred to me: does it matter if it is true?

If the placebo works then, as Seth Godin says, it's even better than normal medicine: all of the benefits with none of the side effects. Beliefs can be like placebos, too. Syed tells the story of Jonathan Edwards, the British athlete who remarkably still holds the triple jump world record more than 20 years after he set it. Edwards was a very religious man while competing, but has since lost his faith. However, even though he is in a very different spiritual and religious place to where he was while competing, Edwards has no doubt that his faith was vital to his success, allowing him to trust in himself and in God in moments when other competitors might have allowed doubt to hamper their performance. He believes this, even though he no longer believes in God.

It made me think of England captain, Harry Kane, who believes, apparently, that each time he misses a chance it makes it *more likely* he will score next time. What I like about this is that it is *almost* true. It is *almost* a reasonable conclusion to draw based on probability. He has an average scoring ratio, and over the course of 10 chances, scores on average a certain number of goals. So, it feels correct to say, 'Well, if on average I score 4/10, and I've just missed one, then there's a 4/9 chance I'll score the next one. More likely!' Except, as any secondary school mathematician will tell you, that's not how it works. It's like flipping a coin: if the coin has come up heads 49 times in a row, how likely is it that it will come up heads next time? 50/50, of course.

Which brings me back to my belief. Does it matter if putting energy out into the world in the build-up to The Coach's Journey is *actually* likely to increase the success of my business in the long term (even if The Coach's Journey doesn't run in 2019)? No. What matters is that I need a belief to keep me resilient and in action during those two weeks, because that is what will dictate the success of the programme.

So, sometimes it doesn't matter if what you believe is true; who knows what is actually true, anyway? It matters if it is useful.

# Chapter Four

# The Problem of Opportunity Abundance

*Written on 21st April, 2017*

Opportunities are out there. If you set your intention for something, then those opportunities will start to present themselves.

For example, if you start looking for somewhere new to live, you will see 'to let' and 'for sale' signs appearing everywhere (there's a reason for this: a part of the brain called the Reticular Activating System).

But the same is true much more broadly. If you set your intention to visit more local shops, you start to notice all the local shops. If you set your intention to have more partnerships, you will begin to see opportunities for partnership appear. If you set your intention to be more sociable, those opportunities appear. But if you take some of the opportunities that appear, there comes a point where you have to decide which new opportunities you have space for. There are infinite possibilities out there, infinite opportunities you *could* take. But you can't take them all.

And what an amazing problem this is to have. What a problem of abundance. How far you've come from thinking you needed more partnerships, more social interaction, more chances to shop local… to thinking you have too many. Well done for coming this far.

But how do we make those choices? I used to feel my way, asking myself, 'Does it feel good to keep this opportunity progressing?' If so, then I progressed it. If not, then I stopped. But the standards by which I now judge those things must change. When you're unemployed every job looks great. When you're lonely, every personal interaction is so valuable. When you aren't, things are different.

And we struggle to say no. We struggle with the guilt of moving from *have not* to *having in abundance*.

Marie Kondo's system of reorganising your home rests on two concepts. First, to discover what are the things that spark joy? And second, if things do not spark joy, to let them go with gratitude. Perhaps those two concepts – sparks of joy and letting go with gratitude – are the answer to more than reorganising our homes. After all, we don't just live in a world of material abundance. We live in a world of opportunity abundance too.

So, let go of the opportunities that are there with gratitude, and get focused on what matters.

# Chapter Five
# The Struggle to Say 'No'

*Written on 12th April, 2017*

Saying 'No' is hard. Or at least it is for me. Some things I have struggled to say no to recently include meeting a friend I haven't seen for a while when I'm really tired; a client who would like to work with me but who I don't feel I will do great work with; a meeting with someone who wants to speak to me when I have a lot on and need some time to myself.

As I look at these problems, I notice that they are problems of abundance. I have too many people I'd like to see, too many things I'd like to do. I have enough clients to be able to say 'No'. What a luxurious position. It reminds me of some of the more practical problems of the modern age. For example, there is so much delicious, cheap food that people can get obese. This just couldn't happen 150 years ago, at least not on the scale it does today.

This doesn't lessen the problem for people suffering from obesity, and it doesn't reduce the strain on the NHS. It is a problem, but it is a problem of abundance. And it is a different and somehow less frightening type of problem than famine.

And so is the problem of saying no, which seems so difficult to me and is causing me stress. More, my inability to do it effectively leaves me busy, worn out and less productive than I could otherwise be.

But this is far less frightening than having nothing to say 'Yes' to. No friends who I'd like to meet and who would like to meet me; no clients to work with (whether we can do 'great work' together or not); no meetings to go to, filled with the possibilities that meetings always are.

And that bears remembering. But so does this: when we struggle to say no, it is usually because there is another commitment. To not forget our friends, to keep ourselves in work no matter what, to stay open to possibilities. That is why we say yes to things, even when it may not be the wise way forward.

So, when struggling to say no, the question must become:

What am I trying to say 'Yes' to?

## Chapter Six

# It's When We Let the Small Things Go That the Big Things Change

*Written on 5th April, 2019*

It always starts small; the little change that, in the end, leads to the whole thing coming crashing down.

You've been really good, giving up sugar for a whole month. The most important thing was kicking chocolate, which you eat like a fiend. Then the month ends and you think, I'll just keep it like this. I feel better, so I'll stay off the sugar.

Then one day, you know you're not on your sugar-free month anymore, so you have something sugary. Just once, just a bit. And then another day it's more, and another day it's more, and a few months later your habits are indistinguishable from how they were before that sugar-free month.

It can be same with habits you have held, even for a long time. You go to the gym regularly. Then you miss it, perhaps because you're injured. After a week or two off because of the injury, you know you'll get back into it. But then that first week back there's a reasonably good excuse – perhaps the dentist, or a visit to the in-laws – which means you can only go once. And you make it once the next week, too, and the week after that. Then one morning you realise you haven't been for weeks or months. The habit has gone. Entirely absent now. And you didn't decide it would be. It's just gone.

Someone once told me that the story of Enron was like that. No one sat down in a meeting and deliberately decided, 'Let's all just agree to act outside of any normal measure of integrity and break the law and screw things up for a lot of people.' Instead, people compromised their values and their integrity, just a little. Then that became the norm. Then those same people compromised their values a little bit more. And in the end, they came to the place where the whole business was sustained by fraud.

These are the things we need to be careful of, in ourselves and in the world at large. Small changes that compound and lead to outcomes no one ever chose.

In *12 Rules For Life*, Jordan Peterson uses Jack Kent's children's book, *There's No Such Thing As A Dragon*, to make this point about our intimate relationships. The story goes something like this. Billy Bixbee notices a tiny dragon on his bed one morning. He tells his parents, who say, 'There's no such thing as a dragon!'. And the dragon grows a little. Billy and his family keep ignoring it and the dragon keeps getting bigger until it has grown so big that it runs away with the house on its back and Billy and his mother inside it; so big now that its head and neck stick out into the street.

Only when the mother and father acknowledge the dragon exists does it shrink back to its original, tiny size. 'I think it just wanted to be noticed,' says Billy.

*I think it just wanted to be noticed.*

In our relationships, we need to name and speak about the small things before, over time, they compound to become the giant, dragon-sized resentments that lead to our marriages breaking down and our homes breaking with them.

But it's not just there. It's everywhere. Every time we see a small transgression, we have the opportunity to notice the dragon and not just pretend it doesn't exist. When someone plays fast and loose with the truth, when someone uses a word a little freely, changing the meaning just a bit, when someone is prejudiced in a pub or in an office... we have the chance to speak up.

And we have the chance to do it in a way that helps, not one that shuts others down. We have a chance to do it with compassion, with the assumption that the person is doing their best and deep down is a good human being, just like deep down we are, even though we don't always behave like it.

This assumption, that the other person is doing their best, is what changes things. It is what, as Brené Brown describes in *Rising Strong*, allows us to hold our boundaries when people are overstepping them, for our good and theirs, without slipping into judgment or resentment. It is what allows us to see things as they are – about us and about others – not as we wish they were.

If we assume that everyone, including us, is doing their best, then we can stop things being about good and evil. We can stop things slipping for others and for ourselves.

We can do it by living as our best selves, but gently, firmly and with courage saying, 'No, this is the line.'

Whether it's allowing the small transgressions that sabotage our good habits, or ignoring the small shifts that undermine our relationships, notice the dragon. Name it and draw a line.

We don't slip any further. You don't slip any further. I don't slip any further.

It ends here. And we are going to stop it.

# Chapter Seven
# This is Life

*Written on 9th August, 2018*

John Lennon was wrong. Life isn't what happens when you're making other plans. Because making plans is life too. *Everything is life.*

Sometimes, after a weekend of 'nothing' – spent recovering or pottering, or just watching Netflix for hours – I think, 'Where does life go?'

But it's a question whose premise deserves to be questioned whenever it is asked. Because *this*, whatever it is you're doing when you ask the question, *this is life*. Right now, this moment.

The normal as well as the extraordinary.

The safe as well as the adventurous.

The things everyone does, as well as the things only you do.

The stability as well as the novelty.

This is life.

I've been craving the normal recently. Wishing for a day when I could just relax. When I could just switch off. Bemoaning my decisions to stretch myself, to lean for bigger things, to dance with Resistance, in life and love, and take my life where I want to. But that… that is just as bad as missing out on life by spending your time planning for the future. Because this – the normal, the abnormal – this is life too. And it needs to be savoured.

There is only one real certainty about life and it's that none of us is getting out of it alive.

And now, wherever and whatever *now* is, this is where life happens. Now, as I write, and now, as you read. This is life. This is, in fact, all there is.

The past has happened, the future isn't real and it may never be. All you have is now. All our thoughts happen in this moment, even if they are about the future or about the past. The feelings we have may also seem to stem from other times, but they are only now.

So, whatever you are doing, every day, don't forget: this moment is precious.

Let your distracting thoughts go. Let your regrets about the past go. Let your worries about the future go. Let your resistance of what is actually here now, go.

Bring yourself into the moment. And choose how you will use it.

So, where does life go? It doesn't go anywhere. This – now, here – *this is life*.

# Part Two: DEAL WITH YOURSELF

You will try and stop yourself. You will try and give up. You will procrastinate and resist the things that on some deeper level you know you want to do. All the great thinkers on creativity will tell you that.

As I wrote in *How to Start When You're Stuck*, the only thing that's stopping you is *you*. And when we're starting, we need to remember that, because that allows us to take that first magical step.

But when we're thinking about the long haul, as we are in this book, when we're thinking about sticking with our practice, every day or week or month, for years. Then it becomes even more important. You don't just need to remember that the things stopping you are *all you*, you also need to become an expert at dealing with yourself. In some ways, that's what all the 12-Minute Method books are about. How do you deal with yourself so that you can make the work that is calling to you?

And here, when we think about keeping going, about persisting, about not giving up, is where it starts to get serious. Where we need to think about practising dealing with ourselves; need to think about making ourselves an expert in our own methods of sabotage, in our own fears and worries. An expert in the things that make humans human, and the things about humans that don't always work for us when we want to create something.

Maybe you're someone who can just make the commitment to themselves and know they'll keep it. If you are, fantastic. Go off and create.

If you know you'll wobble, then welcome to the club. That's what Part Two is here to help you with: it contains a set of ideas, actions and frameworks to remind you of your humanity, to help you accept it and work with it. To give you ways to practise developing yourself, so that you'll be less likely to give up next time, and even less the time after that. To help remind you that you're you, and that's okay. And you need to keep going anyway, despite all that.

Read it looking for the insights that will help *you specifically* deal with *you specifically*. Find the inspiration to be your own coach, your own psychologist, so that on those days when giving up is only a millimetre away, you can catch it, catch yourself, sit back down and keep going.

# Chapter Eight

# We Are the Storytellers of Our Lives

*Written on 25th October, 2018*

We don't always realise it, but within us is the power to change our story: to see things differently and to shift from a place where we are a victim of circumstance to a player in the game of life. To shift from *Life Happening To Me* to *Life Created By Me*.[1]

I was talking to a friend recently about the restrictions she had on her time to see coaching clients, because of her responsibilities as a parent. It felt like a challenge to only be able to see clients on one day a week. Could she support them? Was that enough to offer them? What if they weren't free on Tuesdays?

But what if the story is different. What if, instead, she is a coach who creates her life first, then creates her business to support the woman she is? What if only being able to see clients on one particular day each week isn't about her failures as a coach, but about her power and success as a creator, as a player in the game of life? What if she is a role model for other players, and a sign that the dream – a business that allows you to do all the things outside it that fulfil and enrich and matter – is possible?

And what if only having three slots a week to see clients actually makes her more attractive to clients, who want to work with someone who models that kind of whole-life success? And it will certainly change who she wants to work with. If there is only space for six clients at once, then she is suddenly in a place of choice – a player – when it comes to the work she accepts.

This is an important thing to remember. And it is a hard thing to remember. One of the core principles of my future book, draft title *The Power to Choose*, is that we can be the storyteller in our lives. We can choose our own adventure. We can change how we see things and create a new story.

Sometimes, the story of the victim is important. It's how we cope and deal with what life throws our way. And often it seems safer and easier. Because being a player, a creator, comes with responsibility. If I can choose, then all this, all of life, is *down to me*. It is my fault, as well as my success.

Within this responsibility also comes freedom. It doesn't feel like we live in a world of responsibility most of the time in this day and age. We are surrounded by blame and judgment: the others out there whose fault our circumstances are. It may even be at least partly true; we may be massively affected by others. But is that the story that will help us change things?

Is there another story – just as true, but more useful, more empowering – that you can tell? What happens for you if you change your story? It can make a difference straight away, the rush of seeing the world differently, or it can take weeks or months to come to terms with a new story. To embody it.

But *what if*? What if life is a series of stories you are telling yourself? What if there is a new story out there that changes everything? And what if you have the power to tell it?

## Notes

---

1. As I wrote in *How to Start When You're Stuck* the *Life Happening To Me/ Life Created By Me/ Life Happening Through Me/ Life Happening As Me* framework, which I first read about in Jim Dethmer, Diana Chapman and Kaley Warner Klemp's book, *The 15 Commitments of Conscious Leadership,* is a powerful tool for thinking about ourselves and how we are responding to life.

# Chapter Nine
# I Am What I Am

*Written on 29th April, 2019*

On Tuesday I got out of the shower in an Airbnb in Edinburgh and pulled on the clothes I had brought with me from London to wear for the first of two days of workshops I was facilitating.

I looked at myself in the mirror and felt a rising feeling of anxiety as I considered the clothes I was wearing: whether they were OK, whether they were appropriate, whether they would convey what I wanted to convey, whether they would help me create the kind of first impression on these 24 leaders that I wanted to create.

I stood there, looking in the mirror for several minutes, wrestling with the feeling, wondering if I should change. Am I too smart? Should I put jeans on instead? Am I too scruffy? Should I re-iron this shirt?

From deep within me, the words came. I looked in the mirror, and thought, *I am what I am.*

I shrugged my shoulders. *I am what I am.*

I am not someone who is deeply polished. I am not someone so professional they would wear a suit. Neither am I some tech genius in Silicon Valley, comfortable and proud in a hoodie and trainers. I am what I am.

These clothes are a reflection of me; me exactly now, with all my crumples and insecurities. They are absolutely the best choice I could make right now, by virtue of being the choice I made. I am what I am.

The day went well. My clothes fitted and I felt like myself. In fact, I felt I was more present than usual in that kind of role in front of a group.

And, the next morning I stood in front of the mirror again. This time, I was wearing a slightly different outfit. My shirt was more crumpled, or the crumples just showed up more because of the colour. I stood there again; the feeling of anxiety was even stronger.

*I am what I am.*

I am the kind of person who irons a shirt, but sometimes runs out of patience or prioritises other things and doesn't quite manage to get it pristine.

I am what I am.

I am in good shape. But I am not perfect. I am crumpled and rough around the edges.

I am what I am.

I care. I am not careless or fancy-free. But I am not pristine. Sometimes, I take a step forward before I am pristine. And, almost always, it works.

Whether the shirt is crease-free, the email is typo-free, the speech is stutter-free, the video is confusion-free, or not, I do step forward.

I do leave the room. I am not trapped there by inaction. I step out.

And like every time, life goes on.

I am what I am. If people don't like me, don't trust me, because of what I am, then there's nothing I can do about that. If they trust me because my shirt is ironed pristinely, then they aren't trusting me, they are trusting the shirt. I am not pristine, and I don't want to pretend to be.

But if they trust the man with the shirt that is crumpled at the shoulder, then that's different. That's trusting *me*, the real me.

I am what I am.

# Chapter Ten
# When Our Nerves Are Lying

*Written on 12th July, 2017*

*Nerves. Feeling nervous.* The words are evocative but not as impactful as the feeling itself, if you can conjure it up inside yourself now.

Your nerves, the things that control the sensations in your body, are on edge. Your nervous system is on alert.

For the majority of the existence of the human race this has been a great safety mechanism, protecting our lives from all sorts of things. Now, mostly, the nerves, the nervousness, come around things that don't really threaten our lives. They still *feel* though.

For me, recently, I've felt my nerves on edge about speaking in front of a group, about a trip away, about whether I'll be able to work effectively away from home (will I let a client down?) and about whether I've double-booked myself with clients.

Now, the interesting thing about this list is that, so far, only one of these has actually happened. Further to that, only one of these has been something that I *knew* was going to happen. This was a fun (it turned out) workshop I ran for The Coaching School.

The others were all imagined future problems, leading to my nerves jangling and anxiety firing like I was faced with a tiger or a snake.

This is an important distinction to make: feeling nerves, feeling anxious, feeling fear isn't a bad thing. As David Gemmell says, fear is there to keep you alive. These days it's not necessarily keeping you alive, but it is keeping you on your toes and that can be incredibly useful when you're facing some public speaking or a job interview. But feeling anxious and nervous about possible futures, things that may never happen, well that's not much use at all.

So, what to do? The first part, I think, is awareness. Then, if you want a really practical suggestion, Tim Ferriss' TED Talk on Fear Setting gives a method I really like for first quantifying and then mitigating your fears.

But mainly, just remember to distinguish between the fear of things that *will* happen and the fear of things that *may* happen. They aren't the same thing.

# Chapter Eleven

# The Words We Use Matter – To Us and To Society

*Written on 28th February, 2019*

I have seen this truth many, many times: the words we use matter.

We need, therefore, to be careful which words we choose.

I have written elsewhere of the power (in making me feel less busy and stressed) of stopping complaining about time. It turns out that starting every email with 'I'm sorry for the delay...' makes me feel guilty and rushed because, essentially, I subconsciously assume that the words I am using are true.

Try it for yourself. Put yourself on what Gay Hendricks calls a strict diet of not complaining about time.

Or sit and think about something that is coming up that you are apprehensive about: a social engagement perhaps, or a meeting in your diary.

Try saying to yourself a few times, 'I *must* go that meeting' or 'I *have* to be at that party'.

What happens in your body? What does it feel like?

Then try again with 'I *choose* to go to that meeting' or 'I *choose* to be at that party'. See what that feels like.

If you're like most people, there will be a difference. The words we choose to think and speak create the world we experience as our brain and body react to those thoughts and that speech. It might, again, be the Reticular Activating System of our brain filtering what it thinks is important to you (noticing pregnant women everywhere when we are expecting a baby, or 'For Sale' signs everywhere when we are looking for a house. There aren't suddenly more pregnant women or 'For Sale' signs, it's just that your brain shows you more). It might also be that when we tell ourselves we don't want to do something our body *feels* uncomfortable doing that thing. It might be that we begin feeling guilty *because* we're beginning to believe that we 'should have replied earlier' to an email. Our experience of reality may be shifting *because* of the words we use.

Language matters to others, too. We have a responsibility to choose our words wisely not just for ourselves, but for society.

Today, I saw a man on Twitter labelling a British politician a 'fascist'. Now I accept that my contact doesn't like the politician and, in these charged times, many might agree with him that the man in question is very dislikeable. But this MP is by no rational definition a fascist.

To suggest he is, seems to me a grave disrespect to the victims of fascism in the 20th century and today.

Why does this matter? It matters because I know he isn't a fascist and so should my contact, rationally. And so would everyone who read his comment if they were to stop to think. But as a society, something changes when we throw that accusation around, when we are not careful with our language. The meaning of the word changes. My contact, and his contacts, may begin to *believe* this man is a fascist, believing fascists are everywhere; their sense of reality may shift as a result.

In my case, aware of this dilution of the language, when I hear someone accused of being a fascist, I am not sure whether they are a full-on supporter of the Nazi party, or whether they are a democratically elected Member of Parliament who might have some disagreeable views on Brexit but doesn't want to exterminate any races or have dictatorial power anywhere.

I don't have time to do due diligence on the exact views of every person who has a label thrown at them. No one does. Instead, I shortcut. And in this case one of two things happens: either I (often) wrongly assume someone has far more disagreeable views than they do (that they are a racist, or a fascist, or a homophobe, when the truth is far more nuanced) or I consciously, or more likely unconsciously, stop trusting accusations of fascism.

And this happens to us all. We become desensitised to those words, as they are thrown around. They cease to have meaning. It means that when a genuinely heinous person arrives in our midst, the words we have to describe them, to call alarm, have been relieved of any notable meaning.

And for all of us, if we are careless with our language, our sense of reality shifts, our sense of what is true in the world is diluted. And what, then, are we to base our decision-making on?

So be careful with your words. Be precise. Accuracy matters. Truth matters. To us, and to our society.

# Chapter Twelve

# Worry: A Scourge of Our Times

*Written on 6th April, 2018*

Ah, worries. What a scourge you are.

Last night I was worried. I looked at my diary for today and it was busy. A call in the morning, just one hour between that and my next call, an hour in which I would need to eat lunch and prepare. Then a short gap and another call. Then a short gap... and another call. Not only that, but none of these were ongoing clients where everything works itself. Instead they were a mixture of prospective clients and new clients. All required thought, energy and preparation. There was no time for me to breathe between calls, let alone prepare. And I've been ill. I've been sick for about two months, with one or two or three colds or viruses draining me. I've needed time between calls. I've needed long breaks, sometimes naps during the day. And these calls mattered: they were new and prospective clients who I was excited about. I wanted to work with them (if that was the right thing for us to do). I wanted it to go well.

So, I worried. I did some preparation late into the night. I didn't mind too much as it was interesting, but even at my best a day like today would stretch me to the edge of my energy. And my worries kept me up late; even the latest novel of my favourite author couldn't switch my brain off until about 1.00am. So, less sleep, less energy, and more worry.

And then today. My first call ended, perfectly, 45 minutes early. Suddenly time was opening up. My second call was postponed. More time. Time for lunch, time to chat with my sister. Time to read more of my book.

And my energy is there. Touching wood, perhaps I'm on the mend. At the very least, I have the energy for today.

And, in this case, suddenly, there is nothing to worry about. Three calls instead of four, enough energy to manage them. One done, and beautifully done. Two done, three done.

But what about that energy from yesterday? That wasted energy of worry.

What a scourge it is.

Gay Hendricks, in his book *The Big Leap*, says worry is one of the biggest signs of our Upper Limit Problem. That is, the systems and patterns we create for ourselves that hold us back from happiness. Want to check if you have an Upper Limit Problem, sabotaging you from being as happy as you could be? Worry is a good way to check.

Now, not all worry is bad. In my case, some of the worry got me doing the preparation last night, which made me more prepared, particularly in the event that no calls were cancelled. That worry set me up for a good day, with or without a cancellation.

But some is bad or, at least, a part of our Upper Limit Problem. Here's how you check which kind of worry it is.

First, is it a *real worry*? i.e. Is what I am worried about based in the real world?

Second, is there *anything I can do to affect it* and mitigate it?

For instance, I am worried I haven't locked my front door, and it doesn't have a catch so it might be standing open (this was a real worry of mine in 2011). This is a *real worry;* it is a problem *in the real world.* I've left it unlocked before and it's risky because a lot of people walk past my front door. And *there is something I can do to affect it.* My friend Fergus walks to work past my house. I texted him and asked him to check. He was just walking past as he received the message. The door was locked. And if it wasn't, he could have helped.

Thank you, worry. That was useful.

But how about this one? It's a common one among coaches and I caught myself doing it today:

'What if I do all these things that might connect me to great clients and then I end up with too many clients?'

I kid you not, several coaches I have worked with have shared this with me. I have felt it. *I felt it today.*

Now if that isn't an Upper Limit Problem, I don't know what is. I am worrying about that, about having too many clients, and perhaps I am even doing things to mitigate it, to *stop myself* getting too many clients. In the real world, the opportunity to work with more clients – or refer them to other professionals – is an exciting thing. The kind of thing that makes me happy. And, of course, it's not even in the real world: I have the capacity to work with more clients. So, I am just wasting energy on worry. Now I'm better at dealing with worry than I used to be, and I caught that one early, snorted at my own ridiculousness, and moved on.

But I'm not always able to do that. I've done a lot of work on it and *still* I'm not always able to do it. And here's the thought: *what would the world be like if we could lift the population out of and away from the scourge of worry*?

Even if we just relieved everyone of 10 per cent of the energy they expend on worries outside of the real world or outside their sphere of influence, how much happier would we be? What might we do with that energy? What might the world be like?

So, catch yourself in those moments of worry. Ask yourself those questions. And trust that the universe will probably give you a gift to make it a perfect day anyway. Perhaps a cancellation. Perhaps light at the end of a tunnel of illness.

And, even if 'it' happens, it's almost never as bad as your worry tells you.

# Chapter Thirteen

# Frustration

*Written on 3rd February, 2017*

Frustration is a tough thing to deal with. It shows up at unexpected times, on a big and a small scale. For me, one of the most common times is when things don't work for me. When I can't find something in its normal place, when technology doesn't work as I expect it. When things don't go as smoothly as they *should*.

I find it surprisingly hard, for example, when getting incredibly frustrated that my laptop doesn't work, to remember what an amazing and wonderful thing it is that laptops work at all.

And the same is true with my frustration with people. Frustration is almost always because they don't behave in the way that I think they should. They don't know what I think in *exactly* the same way that I do. They behave in a way that really upsets me: they shouldn't do that kind of thing near me!

Frustration, my friend Vegard Olsen says, is a great path to follow to find your values and the things that really matter to you. If you're feeling frustration, then follow it to its root and you will find something you really care about.

Frustration can be useful.

But that doesn't necessarily help you in the moment, when you are (I am) getting incredibly frustrated at not being able to find your medium sized rucksack (it's only a small flat, where the *hell* can it be?!). Or does it?

One of my favourite practices to suggest to clients is that of thanking the voices in our head. Noticing them, remembering they are helpful sometimes – or were once – and saying, 'Thanks for this thought, I know you're trying to help, but it's not what I need now.' It's surprisingly powerful. Maybe it can work with frustration, too:

'Thanks, I know you're trying to help here; you're trying to show me something that really matters and get me closer to it. But not now. Thank you.'

And if that fails? Breathe.

# Chapter Fourteen

# Giving Ourselves the Things We Need

*Written on 5th April, 2017*

*We underestimate what we need. No matter how hard we try to provide for ourselves the things that make us happy, healthy and whatever else it is that we need to live our life in the way that we want, it feels like we have underestimated it. Or maybe it's that we know how much of these things we need but we squeeze them based on other priorities, outside influences.*

*Today, I feel like I'm not delivering to myself some of the things I need to be happy, healthy and excited about my life. There are any number of these that I have discovered over the years and I'm not even sure which I'm not delivering on today.*

Above is what I thought as I walked to my train today. Here are three other possibilities. They may be all true, or they may not be true.

First, the ideas above are a product of the Never Enough world we live in. As Brené Brown says, to see how strong a paradigm this is, all you need to do is notice that everyday millions of people wake up thinking, usually with some frustration, 'I haven't had *enough* sleep'. What more sign do we need that this is an overriding sense in our world?

Second, I have done my best. I'm providing for myself as well as I possibly can. The evolutionary drive to provide those things to ourselves is strong, but there are other strong drives, too. Survival. Duty. Love. And many more.

Third, maybe some days we just don't feel happy. Maybe we've provided ourselves with all the things we need, and independently of that, our emotions haven't fallen into line. Because we're imperfect creatures. We are human, after all.

And sometimes we have to deal with that. Unless we are the mysterious zen type who claims perfect happiness. But I don't believe them anyway. And for the real-deal zen types, it's not about happiness anyway, it's about acceptance.

That, then, is how we deal with it. We accept and we trust. We accept life for what it is – imperfect – and we trust that we know the way forward. My instincts took me to a particular audiobook this morning and it was the perfect time to listen to it. It opened me up and I heard it in a different way to how I would at any other time. And I feel better.

So, listen to yourself. Accept. And trust.

## Chapter Fifteen

# Feeling the Pressure? Look Directly At It

*Written on 26th October, 2016*

I've been feeling some pressure lately and the universe has been sending me messages about how to deal with it.

The pressure doesn't come from a place that is all bad; sometimes the pressure is from things that look really good for me: moving house, weekends full of fun things, work that is outside my comfort zone. But the *feeling* of pressure and stress is still anything but pleasant.

The first sign from the universe came via a coaching client, who in our work has several times mentioned the challenges of negative thoughts. The second was last night during a call with coach and author Jamie Smart on the Coaches Rising Summit. I've been familiar with Smart's work for a couple of years. To give you a brief summary, his work is based on the premise that we think our emotions are telling us about things outside of us: things that have happened, things that will happen, things that could happen – our bank balance, our relationships, our to-do list. In fact, he says, all our emotions ever tell us about is thought taking form in the moment. This is quite a revolutionary idea and is very difficult for some people to get their heads around.

And when I say some people, I include me! It's not that I disagree with Smart's ideas, it's just that agreement doesn't always translate into the kind of embodied knowing that I imagine would release the emotions that aren't helpful to me.

Last night, I asked him a question on the call. What I took away from his answer was that, when you find yourself overwhelmed, preoccupied or emotionally shaken by something, you need to *look directly at* the knowledge that you have about the situation. If all this feeling is about is thought taking form in the moment, look directly at the thought.

Most of us are usually, except in those rare times when we are responding to a really traumatic event, aware that the problems we are anxious about aren't as bad as we think they are. We know that it seems worse late at night; that we will work it out, because, well, we always have up to this point. But that doesn't necessarily relieve the stress.

So, here's my suggestion. Next time you're in that situation, look directly at your knowledge. Use Smart's ideas if that helps, or one of mine, or someone else's. Look directly at your knowledge and see if the feelings pass.

# Chapter Sixteen
# Three Ways to Have More Integrity

*Written on 10th July, 2019*

The truth matters.

Recently in the UK, I've noticed people have been particularly critical of politicians for lying. What I've noticed, though, is that it isn't just the politicians who lie.

Once you make a commitment to telling the truth in your life, things look quite different. I remember talking to a client about this last year. He had been reading *12 Rules For Life* by Jordan Peterson. One of Peterson›s rules (in probably the most profound chapter of a fascinating book) is '*tell the truth—or, at least, don't lie.*'

The client had noticed, after reading this, just how often he didn't quite tell the truth; all these lies were just slipping out. Once he told me about it – and certainly after I later read the book – I started to notice that I was the same. So often, a lie would come out of my mouth without me noticing.

Sometimes it was the lazy usage of a word. Sometimes it was out of politeness, pretending not to know something as a way to hide my gifts or not outshine others. Sometimes it was some weird politeness/obsession with time (apologising for a delay sending emails which weren't that late anyway). But it happened a lot and changing it was hard.

It was hard because it was instinctual. Psychologist Jonathan Haidt uses the metaphor of an elephant and a rider to describe the instinctual and rational parts of the brain. In his book *The Righteous Mind: Why Good People Are Divided By Politics and Religion,* he tells a fascinating story about how his subconscious invented an entirely false story to explain to his wife why he hadn't done the washing up. It was entirely plausible, about the dog and the child and something else, and entirely false. And it was only because he was working on writing about the instinctual and rational minds *at the time* that he even noticed.

So, our instincts sometimes lie before we have even noticed. And it's hard to get an elephant to change direction.

The problem is that integrity leaks out of us when we don't tell the truth and when we give our word and we don't keep it. You know the feeling, the nagging worry: 'I said I'd get back to Robbie by Tuesday and now it's Friday' or 'I said I'd do that thing for my aunt and I haven't, and it's been months now'.

And remember that the language we use to ourselves matters. Again, try saying, 'I get to exercise' instead of 'I have to exercise' or 'I could eat a bit more healthily' instead of 'I should eat a bit more healthily'.

It *feels* different. If our word means nothing – if we aren't truthful – then what do we have? If we don't tell the truth to *ourselves* then how do we know what is real? If we don't tell the truth to ourselves, how can we expect to believe (and keep) the promises we make to ourselves?

Here, then, are three suggestions for bringing more integrity in your life:

- **Tell the truth – or, at least, don't lie.** Do this everywhere you can, whenever you notice it. Notice it in writing, notice it in person. Notice it when speaking to others and notice it when speaking to yourself. The one I'm trying to stop right now is saying, 'see you soon' to people I will almost certainly never see again. *Stop the leaks of integrity.*

- **Make commitments well.** It's hard to keep your word if the commitment you have made is so vague you don't know if you've kept it or not. How do you know if you've kept your word to get back to me if we didn't agree when you would come back to me by? How do I know if I've kept my word to myself if I didn't decide clearly what I would do? *Make commitments that count.*

- **Make amends.** Make a list of all the times you can think of where you haven't kept your word. The book you borrowed and never gave back, the time you stood someone up, the job you said you'd do for your aunt, the £5 you owe Steve, the person you said you'd reply to but haven't. Make the list then work through them. *Honour your word, even if you haven't kept it.*

Develop the integrity that will help you be who you want to be, and keep your word to yourself and to others.

# Chapter Seventeen
# The Dance of Uncertainty

*Written on 12th October, 2017*

I went home this weekend. Not to the new home that my fiancée and I have created in London, but an older home. The former farmhouse I grew up in. And, for the day, an even older home. The Yorkshire market town I was born in, where my parents wheeled me around for my first trip outdoors. Where I took my first steps.

This is both a settling and unsettling experience. There is a feel to that valley where I was born, where the river that I was named after flows, and to the old farmhouse where I lived for many years. A connection. This is where I came from. It settled me.

And it unsettled me.

I won't be back there soon. I'm going to the other side of the world. It's an adventure, but I don't feel adventurous. I think of those places, of the visceral feeling they give me. My places. Connections deeply felt, going back decades. As I think of those places, I feel scared. Going to a place where I have no connection, where I don't even know what is legal and what isn't.

And uncertainty is unsettling.

My father shared some wisdom with me this weekend, as he has so many times over the years. This time it was the wisdom of Ken Wilber: that really life is just a balance between stability and novelty, familiarity and unfamiliarity; between certain and uncertain, settled and unsettling.

That is the dance, in each moment.

Too much certainty and we are bored, unchanging, unlearning, ungrowing. We are stagnant. Unfulfilled.

Too much uncertainty, and we lose ourselves.

Don't fly too high, Icarus. But don't fly too low, either.

Stretch yourself, but look after yourself.

Change yourself, but remember yourself.

Be yourself, but remember that you can change. You will change. You are changing.

There the dance is.

# Chapter Eighteen

# The Secret to Our Happiness is Within Us

*Written on 17th November, 2017*

Oh no. I think they were right. I think maybe it is all inside. All of it. I think that in each of us – *in* us, not outside – lies the secret to our happiness.

I've heard them telling me, since I was young. And I didn't believe. I *heard*, but I didn't *believe*.

What if it's all here? What if there really is a gift in every moment? In every experience? What if that isn't a load of zen crap?

Well, then the possibilities are endless.

Oh, I should have known. I should have known. My mother was part of a Buddhist organisation for almost as long as I can remember. My dad studied to become a dharma teacher and exposed me to mindfulness long before it became the buzzword it is today. And I didn't see it.

I don't blame myself. I just notice it.

Because something has changed for me recently. And it's one of those stories that I just didn't used to believe. I used to shake my head a little, smile, snort.

In September, I got a cold. I hate being ill. I hate that it restricts me. I hate that I'm not at my peak physical health.

I hate that I can't do everything I want to do. But this time I decided to do something different. I'd been writing about decision and choice. And I thought, I wonder what happens if I decide to *not* hate being ill this time. I wonder what happens if I decide to *enjoy* it. And here's what happened: being ill, it turns out, was fine. In fact, in telling this story to some of my clients I couldn't help but laugh, and the laughter made me happy. And the illness didn't seem to last that long.

It turns out it wasn't the illness that caused my suffering; it was *me*, resisting the illness.

A few weeks ago, I was on a call as part of a Coaches Rising training course. There was a technical problem and 20-30 people were stopped from getting onto the call. Jim Dethmer, the teacher, had been telling some kind of 'old fashioned zen story' about *'What if what is happening now is perfect? What if each moment is perfect?'*

Then Joel Monk, facilitating the call, shared the technical mistake he had made and Iveta, a participant who had been unable to get on the call, spoke, almost in tears at the injustice and frustration of missing out. Dethmer unpacked it with them and what unfolded was a beautiful, vulnerable and affecting change in everyone on the call. How could it be true that anything could be a gift, could be the perfect thing to be happening in this moment? Well, here was an impossible thing to be grateful for: a technical cock-up which cost 20-30 people a few minutes of something they had paid for. But for everyone on the call, that cock-up led to a perfect demonstration of how each moment is perfect. For Iveta, held off the call, something magical happened, too. Even as I write this, I notice my own reticence to share it. I'm worried you won't understand, that my explanation is imperfect. But thanks to Dethmer's practice, taught to us in that session, I can see that is just my own desire for control, for approval, for security. What if this article is perfect, just the way it is?

What does this mean for me? It means that two days ago I could sit, as I got ill again, and *thank* the world for the gift of the illness, which took me to my bed and my fantasy novel. Well, not quite. But I can suffer so much less, and read my book, and be loved for who I am. And you know what? I got better yesterday. Almost completely recovered, within 24 hours. What a gift.

I think they were right. I think they were right, all along. The secret to our happiness is within us. It is in our choices, it is in our awareness, it is available.

And although it is within us, that doesn't only affect what is inside. I heard psychologist Ellen Langer this week, talking about how acting younger actually made some people in her experiment *look* younger. I have seen, first hand, how changing things inside can create incredible power outside, in the world.

And, as I sit in gratitude, as I reflect on this. I am filled with a tiny bit of 'oh no'. A tiny bit of, 'I shouldn't have been so sceptical.' A tiny bit of 'what could have happened if I knew this earlier; really *knew* it?'

But mostly I am filled with joy. Because I think this is coming, for all of us. And it is within our grasp.

# Part Three: NEGOTIATE THE ONLINE COMPARISON TRAPS

The online world has changed things. And there's no going back.

Those changes are what makes this book, this series, worth writing. It is now possible for everyone – *everyone* – to create change around the world, without needing the permission of anyone else. You, yes *you*, can start a business, write a book, have your own TV channel and more. And all you need is a phone and an internet connection.

And, we aren't designed for a world where we are connected to everyone. We evolved to live in small communities, to take our places in groups of 150 or less (according to some people, at least).

When we're in a group of billions, all connected together, strange things begin to happen. Suddenly it is essentially impossible for us to stand out, to be 'the best' at anything, whereas in previous centuries to find and feel the uniqueness of our position in the world was far more possible. Being the most competent grocer you know of was within your grasp when we rarely travelled more than a few miles. It would only take five minutes on the internet for most of us to find someone who does what we do but is 'more successful' than we are.

And this is one of the most insidious moves of the

quitting monster. It's got to me, and it's probably got to you too. Quitting (or not starting) because of all the people out there you can see doing what you want to do.

'There's no point doing this when X is much better at it than me,' was bad enough when I was at school. With the internet to constantly show me cleverer, more successful, richer, more attractive versions of me, comparison becomes a trap that is almost impossible to resist.

And yet, if we're going to keep going, we have to resist it. That's what Part Three is here for. It's not long, but it's important. These lessons stay with me more than most in this book, shoved in my face every day by the internet. In them, I'll share what I've learned about resisting those online comparisons. Not resisting them completely, of course, but enough so that I don't give up. So that I remember that I'm me, and I'm still unique even if there are countless people out there doing something similar to me.

Even if there are those people, even if they might be doing it better than me, that doesn't mean I should give up. Because it's not about me. It's about who I might become if I don't give up. And it's about how my work might change people if I make it and share it.

It only needs to change one person for it to be worth it.

So, resist the comparisons.

You're unique. You're wonderful. You're doing great work. And I don't want you to quit.

Resist.

# Chapter Nineteen

# We Keep Going Until We Create Something That Is *Ours*

*Written on 18th May, 2018*

I went to a festival last weekend. Punk-folk singer-songwriter Frank Turner took over the Roundhouse in Camden for four glorious days of music and great company. I left it feeling in awe of what the man had created. All four evenings – Turner (sometimes with his band) playing a set each night – were sold out. 3,000 people, four nights in a row. That in itself is incredible, considering that when I first saw him live 10 years ago, he was playing to rooms of a few hundred.

But it was more than that. These crowds of people he had brought together through a love of his music were a truly beautiful group of people. So diverse in so many ways, but all incredibly friendly and kind. And, these concerts *mattered* to them. There's almost nothing like being in a room of 3,000 people, all singing together. At Frank Turner gigs, this happens partly because Turner encourages it ('There are two rules for my gigs. Number one: don't be a dick. And number two: if you know the words, sing!') and partly because this music matters so much to these people. The humanity and wisdom in his words has changed the lives of so many of them, just as it has mine.

The festival was such a beautiful experience, lifting me in ways that very few things can. And, it showed me starkly the scale of the work that is possible for a human being. It is possible to create something that matters *that much* to thousands of people.

And the festival left me adrift with my own work. Because how can I ever create something that matters *that much* to *that many people*? I am so far from that.

This is a trap I fall into so often. A trap of comparison. Because the answer is almost certainly that I can't. I will almost certainly never (although you can never be sure!) create a festival at somewhere as big as the Roundhouse that matters *that much* to *that many people*. And at that point there is a part of me that wants to give up. If I can't create something like that, then what's the point? I might as well stop now. And, more than that, the journey of entrepreneurship is hard and unforgiving. So, if I can't create something like that, perhaps it's time to stop and do something different, something easier.

Except that the story of Frank Turner shows the falseness of that comparison.

Turner first achieved success in punk band Million Dead. His lyrics, the energy of the Million Dead live shows, and their great music took him and his band to success in the scene, and the edge of much more. Before it came crashing down.

And then he started again. With something different. I've heard him tell it differently, but either after listening to Bruce Springsteen's Nebraska and Johnny Cash, or at a prod from one of his friends, he set off in a very different musical direction. And he didn't set out to create Lost Evenings at the Roundhouse. He set out to play his songs, wherever and whenever he could. His criteria were something like, 'I'll play anywhere if I get £50 and a place to sleep'. And he played, and he played, and he played. And each time, because he did the best work he could, he picked up a few fans. And every now and again, his work touched someone, like me, who would be so affected by his work that they would be going to four shows in a row at a festival in Camden around a decade later.

And then, after many years, as he continued to play and play and play, things moved. His work touched enough people that the industry started to take notice. And, in the end, this took him to the Roundhouse. And by this time, he had mastered his craft. He had found his audience.

So, we keep going. We keep learning and playing. Until we create something. Something that matters. Something that is not theirs. We can't make *that*. That's Frank's, or it's yours, or it's hers or it's his. It's not mine. So, we keep going. Until we create something that is *ours*.

This life I've created… well, it's definitely not perfect. But I've yet to figure out a better way to spend my time.

When I do, I'll change. Until then, I'll keep going.

# Chapter Twenty
# The Internet Comment Trap

*Written on 30th September, 2018*

There's a feeling I get. In fact, I've got it now. I used to get it much more, but it's still there on days like today.

It is nicely summed up by a little cartoon I saw a few years ago of a man hunched over his computer. His wife called down from upstairs: 'Come to bed, darling, it's late.'

'I can't come up yet,' he replied. 'Someone on the Internet is WRONG!'

While the cartoon is funny, the feeling is not. It can range from frustrated and angry to upset and anxious, for me at least. There's a kind of righteousness in it, sometimes.

I'm in it now because someone commented on something I wrote. There was criticism in what she said, and I feel misunderstood. I'm tired, too, which doesn't help. And this piece, in particular, carried vulnerability – about a new piece of work I have recently launched – and, deep down, I know it's a little more controversial than most of the things I write or share. I knew when I wrote the piece that some people wouldn't like it. That's why I've procrastinated on it; shied away from it for so long. Maybe where the feeling comes from, really, is that the comment played into the doubts I had myself. Am I the right person to do this work?

Or not? Maybe that's where this feeling always comes from: a fear that I might be wrong; of being caught out.

I was having dinner with someone once who was being quite argumentative. Later, someone shared, 'It didn't feel like they were arguing with us; it felt like they were arguing with someone else, or themselves, from long ago.'

Maybe this is what is happening when we feel this rising feeling. I have watched others dealing with this, particularly those with big Twitter followings, and wondered if they feel the tension I do when people are disagreeing with them. And mostly, over time, I've come to the conclusion that they sometimes do, and they sometimes don't. And that if sometimes they don't, then there must be something we can do to practise engaging in conversations over the Internet in a way that doesn't leave us feeling a kind of tension that we don't like.

But also, they are human, so mostly they probably do feel that. At least a bit. I don't feel it as much as I used to. I find that I can enter into these kinds of internet conversations about my work and other things with much more freedom and ease than I used to. But, each time, at first I have to breathe through it. Perhaps to remember that they aren't arguing with me, but with themselves, or something else from another time.

And, as far as I can tell, the greater ease partly comes by sharing *more* of my truth with the world than before, as I have done a couple of times this year, and not by hiding and allowing fear to grow.

# Chapter Twenty-One

# We Look a Lot More Successful Than We Are and We Are A Lot More Successful Than We Feel

*Written on 2nd February, 2018*

Something came to me this week; a strange thought, that feels slightly paradoxical: we *look* a lot more successful than we *are*. But we *are* a lot more successful than we *feel*.

## We look a lot more successful than we are

Of course we do. We live in the world of social media, where we almost always share online only the sexiest pictures of ourselves, the most glorious shots of us in sunny places, babies looking happy, children looking cute, our cats playing, hilarious thoughts we've just had, the programmes we've launched, our business successes, great testimonials, our engagements and our weddings. Occasionally, we post about something bad, but usually it's about how shoddy someone else has been to cause our misery or how our misery has become a glorious success. We almost never post about our misery itself.

Imagine if we did. Imagine if a different social media existed: incredibly unsexy photos, us huddling in a doorway in Costa Rica in a tropical rainstorm wishing we weren't bloody freezing and could just be back in England where the rain is normal. Babies screaming, children looking infuriating as they smash up stuff and cause chaos, cats hissing or destroying our sofa, dull thoughts we've had (let's face it, that is most of them). The programmes we launched for which we don't sell a single place, the business failures, the terrible (or worse, incredibly average) testimonials, breakups and divorces. These things don't show up on social media. We do these things quietly. And maybe that's a good thing. We don't want to always share our failures with the world and that's fine.

But it creates a paradox. We see how successful other people are and we compare what's going on for them on social media with what's going on for us in *real life*. And in real life, all the things in the paragraph above happen. So, it's not a fair comparison.

### We are a lot more successful than we feel

We spend so much time comparing ourselves to others in this incredibly unbalanced way that we develop a twisted version of our own success. We mostly don't hear about successful celebrities and business people talking about how they can't sleep, how they worry, how six businesses fail before any succeed. We get wrapped up in our own failures, our own struggles. The way companies in Silicon Valley and elsewhere have embraced failure as a route to success may have changed that somewhat, and it is probably true that there are great stories of failure out there. And listening to Tim Ferriss and working with Rich Litvin reminds me that there are people out there trying to talk about the struggles.

But most of us don't realise that. Because the business failures that get talked about tend to be the ones that come before great success and maybe our great success hasn't come yet. Because we see the sunny holiday and we think about how we're failing because we can't afford to do one this year. Or we see the engagement and we think, 'I'm 33 and I'm never going to meet anyone.' Or we see the successful career path and think, 'Hell, I'm never going to have that.'

We twist our success in comparison and so we almost certainly *are* more successful than we feel.

## No one can compete with you at being you

But here's the thing. Other people are twisting their success in comparison to you: thinking about how successful *you are* and being intimidated. I bet they are. You don't believe me, but they almost *have to* think that, unless you never talk about your successes. Remember, inside almost all of us is the voice telling us we're not good enough, trying to keep us safe and hidden. And we are really good at comparing ourselves to others. Competition is one of the things that has driven us onto greater and greater achievements as a species. But when competition stifles us because of the unbalanced view we take of the world, coupled with our internal stories, then it isn't helping. So, here's the thing to remember.

No one can compete with you at being you. So, find that thing – the thing that only you can do. Take your failures, take your successes. Be a professional, and give them the weight they deserve – and they both deserve weight. Then do the things that only you can do, bringing the gift and experience that only you can bring.

*You look more successful than you are.*

*You are more successful than you feel.*

*And no one can compete with you at being you.*

# Part Four: DON'T LOSE HEART – LESSONS FOR THE DARK DAYS

There will be days when keeping your promises to yourself will be easy. But that won't be all the days.

If you plan to stick with something, to keep going, to make something over years of work, then there will be difficult times. That's life. That's being human.

Bad things happen in our lives. Dark days. And sometimes they are followed by even darker ones.

If we want to persist, to keep going over years, we need to know that. We need to accept it and prepare for it. That's what Part Four is about. It is about (and sometimes written during) the dark days.

It is here to let you know that's normal. And it's my letter of appreciation to all the people out there who have displayed the persistence, the courage, the bloody-mindedness to sit down and create even on the darkest days.

To keep showing up, even as the shadows lengthen and the walls draw in.

On those days, don't lose heart. Some of the greatest works of business, of art, of creativity, have undoubtedly come from those places. Some of the things that changed the world most were born in the darkness.

And sometimes the biggest personal transformations I have seen in myself and in my clients have come from those dark places too.

The darkness is a part of the journey, a part of life.

If we can develop the courage to show up even on those darkest days, then really, what can stop us?

# Chapter Twenty-Two
# The Hero's Journey of Growth

*Written on 5th September, 2019*

I was thinking earlier today about the trapeze. I've never seen expert trapeze artists in person but (because of my partiality to a Batman comic as a young man and my knowledge of his sidekick Robin's origin story) it feels like I've always been aware of them.

Here's what I was thinking: it takes incredible daring and there must be almost nothing like the moment when you are in the air, having let go of a trapeze. Your experience and training tell you that you will reach out and catch the next trapeze. But for that moment, suspended in the air above the circus floor, what must that be like?

Then, I realised, I know a little about what it's like.

At a workshop I recently attended, the psychologist Robert Holden talked about his passion for the Hero's Journey – the archetypal story made popular by Joseph Campbell and more recently by Brené Brown. The Hero's Journey is the cycle that runs through so many of the stories that humans love. It is the origin story of superheroes like Spider-Man, and the plot of almost every (maybe literally every!) Pixar movie. It is *Lord of the Rings* and *The Hobbit* and *Star Wars*.

And it is every story of personal growth.

In the Hero's Journey, the hero leaves their home, steps over the threshold. And in the Hero's Journey, the hero faces darkness. In this moment, the hero is between two trapezes. No matter how many Hero's Journeys we have faced in our lives (and, if you look closely, you will likely find many), in this moment there is a deep fear: *I might not get out of this alive.*

And that is because you won't. The 'you' that started the Hero's Journey, who left the Shire or decided to pursue the person who killed Uncle Ben, is gone once you cross the threshold. The you that sets out on the Hero's Journey will not return. A different you will return, I promise you this. But you can't skip the moment between the trapezes.

In order to cross the threshold, you have to be aware: *this might not work.* I don't know what is going to happen here. You have to let go of the trapeze. Each time you do that in your life, you go through a valve, you see something you can never unsee, you change.

You don't know as you do it that you will catch the other trapeze. You can't. If you know for sure that you are going to catch it, then it isn't a Hero's Journey at all. *This might not work* is a requirement for growth.

But that doesn't make it easy. That doesn't mean the letting go of one's self – the you that left the Shire with the life you had there – is pleasant or easy. In fact, it can be horrible and hard. On the other side, though, you have the thrill of catching the trapeze. I was there, suspended, held by the universe in chaos and openness and *this might not work*. And now here I am, attached to a trapeze again, or standing on the platform with the applause of the audience ringing in my ears.

Adult Development Theory is a field of psychology concerned with the ways that adults' psychology develops over their lifetimes, drawing them into greater perspective and more complex ways of making meaning of the world. Some Adult Development theorists say that our level of development is dependent on what the world asks of us. If the world asks us to step up, then sometimes we are pulled into developmental change. This is what happens in the Hero's Journey: we hear the call. Often, we refuse the call, but it comes again.

We are called to cross the threshold, to see new perspectives. And it feels scary, when the world asks us to step up. It feels uncomfortable. It feels knotty.

You won't get out of that journey alive, at least not the 'you' that enters. But we need you to step up. The world is calling you. Be brave and trust. Trust that supernatural aid will be there when you need it.

# Chapter Twenty-Three
# The Confidence Myth

*Written on 15th March, 2018*

What if this whole confidence thing is a myth? Because I think it might be.

There's a story we're told of the clear, confident person setting out to achieve things and then... well... achieving those things. But for most of us, perhaps with that story in mind, 'I don't feel confident enough' is a thought that becomes rather familiar.

It certainly does for me, yet sometimes I think that any success I have had has been built not on a story of confidence but a story of carrying on despite *not* being confident.

I have been reflecting recently on the power of a part of my adolescence and early adulthood that dominated my life, my friendships, and so many of my experiences since then. It started when I took part in a school play, aged 10 or 11, playing the part of a World War One soldier in the Christmas truce of 1914. Mr Leeming then invited me to take the lead role in the next Christmas play, and for around fifteen years after that I practised the strange art of acting. I took part in tens of productions. And there are two things that come to me now: one is that there were moments in almost every production when I thought it was going to be terrible, that *I* was going to be terrible. The second is that those moments rarely came in the moment just before I stepped out onto stage.

Was I a confident performer? By the end I was. Indeed, I still am. But was I confident the whole way through? No, not in the least. Many a bonding session with a cast was over the soon-to-be-disaster of a production we were in. The terrible leadership. The person who just didn't get it. But mostly, those productions weren't terrible.

And I learnt to carry on. To carry on trying to get better. And, when it came to the moments of truth, to keep going.

On stage, most of the time, I looked confident too. I was playing the game by then. But up until that point, sometimes until the final rehearsals, sometimes even during the productions, I was full of doubts.

What I learnt over those 15 years was that it would be OK. That it was usually better than I thought it would be. That other people (mostly) looked beyond the doubts I had about the production or didn't notice what I doubted. And as for those people who just criticised, criticised and criticised? Well, I didn't have much time for them anyway.

A few months ago, I wrote elsewhere about how, really, confidence is just a belief that you can make happen the things that you want to happen. And that is what I did through those years. I learnt that early in my acting, then it became more and more embodied as I experienced it over and over again.

The worries I had were there to help. They would spur me to find the way to make the character work, to speak up to a director, to speak to a fellow actor to try to make the whole thing better. And over time I learnt that even when the worst happened, it was rarely as bad as I imagined. And I learnt that as long as I didn't stop, things would happen. I would make things happen.

Later, I met Rich Litvin, who introduced me to his much quicker way of saying something very similar, which is perhaps easier for you to remember:

*Confidence is a result, not a requirement.*

So, what am I really saying here? I'm saying that the confident feeling that you desire won't magically appear in the places you want it to. And sometimes the absence of it will feel terrifying.

I'm also saying, why not focus on all the areas in which you *are* confident? You are confident you can climb the stairs to your flat, that you can make your bed, that you can write and send an email, that you can find what you need via Google. There are hundreds of thousands of places in your life where you are, deservedly, confident. You believe through experience that you can make happen the things you want to. You have the result.

And it's almost impossible to remember now the first time you climbed stairs or made a bed. But when you first did it, you didn't know you could. You probably didn't do it well. A fall or a tangled duvet almost certainly happened. But you didn't stop. You just tried again next time. Maybe you learnt a little. And, over time, the confidence emerged.

# Chapter Twenty-Four

# When the World is Closing in on Us

*Written on 5th March, 2018*

Our world is enormous. We are more connected than we have ever been. Almost all of us are, anyway.

And yet sometimes the world closes in.

Like a day when the Internet is down, suddenly our world doesn't feel so big, and we feel somehow trapped, perhaps unable to work. Like a day when snow freezes the roads and the railways and suddenly the size of our world shrinks.

Instead of openness and freedom, our world suddenly feels like a small and frightening place. Each message received feels like it is making the world smaller.

Last week I found my world closing in. Each message I received, each comment online and in real life, felt more like a threat, more like a judgment. There were still glimpses of the openness of reality, but they were fewer and further between. When I saw them, I tried to take the chance to use them, but with the way the world responded, it felt like they just led to the walls of the world getting closer to me still.

The normal ways out didn't work. I was just here, with myself, with the world closing in.

Sometimes I can find my way out of it. Like getting to

the station in the snow to find that trains in the direction you want to go are still running. Or realising that, actually, there's a bus you can take. Sometimes, I just have to wait it out. Retreat. Wait until normality resumes. Wait until reality resumes.

It can be crippling though. For me, these are small things; they last at most a few weeks.

I know someone whose world continued to shrink, and shrink, and shrink. At some point, she couldn't go out of the house very often. Perhaps this was a tactical retreat, to safety and security, like mine last week. To wait for it to pass. But it didn't.

Then, later, she could only leave the house with help. Then it became just once a week. Then, later, not at all. But it's not just the literal ways in which the world can shrink, it's the internal ways. Where trust erodes and assumptions and stories take over. Where, suddenly, everything is a threat and nowhere is safe.

Then the world is so small that we don't even fill ourselves. We exist in only a tiny corner of ourselves. We know, we remember how much we used to fill, but now we can see that our world has closed in on us and left us here.

I count myself lucky, blessed and privileged to only find my walls closing in for a week or two, here and there. At least these days. Maybe it happened more in the past; it's hard to tell. For many this feeling is a far more regular occurrence.

Often these pieces of writing I create, as they emerge, end with something positive: a break, a question to guide us on. Sometimes it comes from my mind, sometimes from my heart, sometimes it emerges as I write from somewhere higher or deeper. I'm not sure that's going to happen today.

The truth is, sometimes our worlds just close in on us. It's so hard. It's hard for us, it's hard for our loved ones, it's hard for our lives and our work.

Perhaps something is, after all, going to emerge today. Because as I sit here, two things come to me. Perhaps the answer to this contraction of our world comes from two places.

Perhaps the answer comes from *curiosity*: from understanding and an opportunity to be curious.

Perhaps the answer comes from *connection*: from love and understanding from another being.

Perhaps those are our weapons, for our loved ones and ourselves, during those weeks, months or years when it feels like the world is closing in around us. Perhaps we won't always win that fight. But we need to try.

So, bring them with you, to your friends and family, to the strangers you meet in a coffee shop and on the street. Bring them to yourself.

# Chapter Twenty-Five
# The Scarcity Trap of Poverty and Debt

*Written on 4th January, 2018*

I did an unusual thing last week: I posted on Facebook about a charity. I don't do this often. Everyone has their own causes and it's up to them to decide which cause is the one that matters to them. But then I got an email through from a charity I support, who had two matching offers on, meaning that every £1 donated by someone like me or you would be tripled by the charity's other supporters. And it felt too important. Because this charity is a little different.

I learnt about them in Rutger Bregman's book, *Utopia for Realists*. Among many interesting perspectives and ideas in that book is a description of a rather startling study, conducted with a group of farmers in India. The seasonal nature of the farmers' work means that they receive 60 per cent of their annual income in a very short space of time. At this point – at the end of their 'season' – they have a good amount of money. Later in the year, they have almost none. And here is the interesting part: the study ran various tests with these farmers at both points. For example, a cognitive ability test. It turns out, when the farmers had lots of money, their cognitive ability was significantly higher than when they had no money. They were literally able to make better decisions.

I'm sure this is familiar to many of you. Most of us have had times in our lives where our debts were high. Maybe the pressure was rent, or a credit card bill, or someone else we owed money to. Or maybe it was just that we weren't making much money. I have had times when my overdraft was high, times when my credit card debts felt overwhelming, and times when my income was so low that my (modest) outgoings were greater than it, and my money was going down and down and down. And it was really hard during those times, in all sorts of ways.

Now consider the consequences of the above study: it is literally harder for us to make logical decisions at those points. There is nothing wrong with us as people; it would happen to anyone.

And this is where the title of Bregman's TED Talk comes from: poverty isn't a lack of character, it's a lack of cash.

And this brings us to the charity, GiveDirectly. They do exactly what they say, they give the money that is given to them directly to some of the poorest people on the planet, making their operation as streamlined as possible, so that 90 per cent of donations go straight to those who need it. These people live on $0.75/day, so donating £1 would more than double the income of one of these people for a day.

And the results of this giving are astounding. I won't go into all of it here, but you can read more on their website about how people don't stop working if you give them money (in fact they seem to work more) and how the results have transformational effects across people's lives, from their work, to their ability to plan for the future, to their relationships with their friends, families and loved ones. This charity is a way to transform the lives of people and it's easy. It's easy because the data is so strong (so you know it really helps). It's easy because you know where the money is going (so if you have that doubt about bureaucracy and poor-quality admin, or money being used for something you don't agree with, you can ignore it here). It's easy because £10 per month to me is less than three pints, but to someone in the poorest parts of Africa it might double the money they live off for nearly two weeks. And almost every time I find myself thinking deeply about this, I donate some more money to the charity.

This is why I am concerned about poverty *far more* than about inequality. Because imagine what happens each time someone finds their way out of the scarcity space of poverty, anywhere in the world, and is released closer to their full potential. Imagine what we might achieve, what might change. And all it might take is the money to get them out of that scarcity space, to unleash their potential and set them on the upward spiral to whatever awaits them.

And it's also why, at this time of year and at all times of year, if you are struggling with money, then I want you to know you're not alone. Anyone would be finding it difficult, under the kind of pressure you are under. It's so hard.

All we can do in those times is to make the changes we can make. To find, if we can, a way to release the scarcity. To take the next small step on our journey, and it doesn't matter how small as long as it's a step. To remember that change is possible if we can just take action, if we can just keep going.

## Chapter Twenty-Six

# When the Little Decisions Get Harder, It's a Good Sign That Something's Wrong

*Written on 21st March, 2018*

When I'm in good form, I'm a dynamic decision maker. I love sending out emails fast, having decision-making meetings, facing challenges, being in the moment.

At the other end of the spectrum, when I am at my lowest, I can't make any decisions. They just don't come. I slip into a paralysed trap.

With my coach recently, I've been playing with my compass. I have basically followed this compass since I was starting to think about changing careers – the path that, in the end, led me here. I used it first as a way to start breaking the paralysis, to help in the times when there were so many ways I could choose to go that deciding felt basically impossible. How do I choose? Pros and cons won't work because there's no way I can get my rational mind around a decision this complex. So, instead, I trust a very particular feeling and see where it leads; take a step in that direction. If I get more of the feeling from that step, I take another. Then another. If I don't, I stop and go back to the last time I had it. Then take a different step from there.

But it's harder to feel that feeling, to follow that compass, in some situations. It's harder to hear when you're lost in the gremlins and the voices in your head. It's harder to follow when your sense of self-worth is lower.

What I've noticed is that the times when you most need your intuition to guide you are often the times when your intuition seems to disappear. When we're anxious, or depressed. When we are low on money.

So, what do you do? Stop altogether? That doesn't seem quite right.

Leap with no guidance system? That doesn't feel quite right.

Some people (sometimes me) would tell you to just take action. Then the inspiration will be let in.

But the truth is, sometimes inspiration can't get in. Sometimes we are too ill, too poor, too depressed, too anxious.

Then our job is to get through the day. Wait out the storm. Hunker down for winter.

Because spring will come again.

# Chapter Twenty-Seven
# Create the Headspace You Need

*Written on 2nd November, 2016*

This world we live in does fill your head up sometimes, doesn't it?

So many of my coaching clients, at one time or another, have spoken about the need to get more headspace. They have a wide variety of tactics for doing this.

I can remember perhaps the first time that I actively sought to clear my head. I was about 20 and lying in a small room in a very studenty flat on Pentonville Road in London. My head was full of worries and stress. I couldn't sleep and it was late. Very late. I can't remember what I'd already tried, but it was late at night when I settled first upon an album, and then a book. They were a gateway to a simpler period of my life, when the beginnings of adult worries were distant; when the stresses I felt seemed more trivial (to the 20-year-old me, at least).

That wasn't the last time I used that music or that author as a way to pull myself through difficult times. There are of course other techniques I use, too. Chocolate, beer, TV and running are common ones. They work too, but when the going is really tough, that band and that author are, for me, a much stronger tonic of headspace; of wellness. The music of Oasis just sounds like home to me. Those men and that songwriting have been with me since before I really knew what they were singing about, and the inspiration and depth of the words and the melodies, many hundreds of listens later, still hold surprises. And the writing of David Gemmell, a British fantasy novelist who has been so much a part of life that I made a website about the philosophy that runs through his work, has the power to lift me out of the place I am and take me far away. To distract me, yes, but more than that: to relax and inspire me.

These days it usually isn't that band and that writer. I find other bands and other authors (although usually guitar music and usually fantasy novelists) to help me when I need it. And they give me, to a greater or lesser extent, what those artists gave me: not only a means of escape (as so much great art has the power to do) but more than that. They teach me about my humanity. They grow my soul in moments of truth and beauty. Now that sounds like a way to get headspace. A great place to escape to.

# Chapter Twenty-Eight
# Leaning Into Fear

*Written on 8th September, 2017*

Here's a secret: I'm scared. More often than I think. More often than you think, maybe. Not as often as some people, perhaps, but it wells up sometimes. Not as often as it used to, maybe, but sometimes I can feel it. It's a kind of tingling; a sense of the nervous system being on edge. And it's not pleasant. Not the fun nervous-system-on-edge you get before a sporting encounter or stepping onto a stage. Sometimes, though, it's there. And I just want to escape.

As I stand here now, I realise, with a sense of great, almost tear-inducing relief that it really doesn't happen like it used to. There have been times when I have lived so often like that. I'm not sure I even knew it, even noticed at the time, but I wonder now how much energy it took to feel out of kilter with who I am, to feel the sense of fear so much.

My fear is often of exposure. It is of being kicked out of the tribe. Found out for the fraud I really am. For the small boy lost somewhere, not sure what to do.

I don't feel it like I used to, but I felt it last night, faced with something new. A different group. A new experience. The possibility of stepping into a new community and a new part of my life.

The tingling of nervousness, the hint of fear... it settled as stories were told, as I learnt about the people sitting around me. I knew it would; I asked for that. In seeing the stories of those people around me, the nervousness settled. At least, I think that's what it was.

And as the nervous system settled, I felt myself able to slip into presence, into the person that I really am. Into something deeper, a deeper wisdom. I don't feel *that* feeling all the time, either, but I feel it more than I used to. And to live in presence and not in fear, in connection and not in competition; that feels like the right shift. For me, but probably for all of us.

It's not easy to do that. I can feel the nervousness rising again now. Time to let it go. That's how we connect, in vulnerability and fear. That's how we learn.

# Chapter Twenty-Nine
# We're Already Moving

*Written on 16th February, 2017*

Here I am. On the train again. Somehow the train is still a rare experience, a period of spaciousness in movement. I'm making such progress towards my goal, in this case London Waterloo, and yet there is also such spaciousness here. An opportunity to savour life in whatever way I want. I can listen. I can read. I can think. I can write.

My desire for progress is satisfied, because I'm moving. I'm slowing now as we're approaching Queenstown Road, but I know I couldn't be getting where I need to get any faster. And so, in the meantime, here I am. Writing to you.

Even the origin of this writing practice came from the idea that these few minutes are a space without pressure. A space where I could do anything. And yet, from there come these articles, which so many people have told me they like.

Is it a coincidence? That the most creative thing I have done in years has come from a time and a place where the pressure is off, where the evolutionary and societal instinct to make the absolute most of my time here, to make the absolute most of my gifts, is postponed by the clear signs of how I'm progressing?

Because there is another evolutionary instinct at play

here: to find space. To feel relaxed. I hear of it so often, from people chasing it.

And a third: to create. Something from nothing. Something that will open my eyes and heart and also touch the hearts and souls of others.

These are strong drives, core desires. To savour life *and* to make the most of it. Mindfulness and progress. Enjoying the moment *and* holding to the almost impossible goals that we know will bring us joy.

Here I am, on the train. I'm moving, even if I'm not *doing* anything to move. I did that thing about 10 minutes ago, getting on this train. And here, now, I'm already moving. I don't have to do anything more. I just have this space. To listen. To read. To think. To write. To live.

I'm already moving, on the train and in life.

We are already moving.

Whatever we are doing.

So, we can, perhaps, relax.

# Chapter Thirty

# Why Do We Keep Asking 'What Next?'

*Written on 27th May, 2018*

When I first wrote these pieces, it was an exercise in how to overcome the incredible Resistance I was feeling to sharing anything online; an almost physical pain and nervousness. Now, 18 months after the first five came out in a two-week period, I have written another almost every week and it feels quite different. Now they come out of me without that physical sensation and pressing 'share' is easy.

Here is evidence that confidence is a result of action, not a requirement to take it.

And then, I notice, I am interested in *what is the next step*? Is it longer pieces? Or perhaps writing on what feels like more controversial topics? One I wrote recently, about responsibility being more important than rights, and the sacred masculine and the sacred feminine, was definitely harder to share. Or is it something that develops my skills further: more criticism and feedback from people to support me developing my writing skills, perhaps. I'm playing with that at the moment, behind the scenes, with a longer writing project I've had on the go for the last 18 months or so.

And then, perhaps because I think too much, the next question comes: *why does there need to be a next step?*

And that is a good question. On her second appearance on the Tim Ferriss Show, master designer Debbie Millman joked about how the kind of success she has experienced is derived in part from the struggles and challenges she has been through. Millman, in her first appearance on the show, talks incredibly touchingly about the trauma she suffered as a girl.

'I think that people who coast through life without ever really feeling impassioned by their work,' she says, 'might just have had really good parenting, and don't feel the need to make a name for themselves by their work because they feel just intrinsically good about who they are.'

And that may be part of it. We are driven on by the stories we were told, implicitly or explicitly, as a child.

But as I sit here, reflecting on the practice that led to this piece of writing, what I remember is that this practice has been *so* valuable to me as an individual. Leaning into that place of pain and fear, with the help of my coach, led to this practice: a desire to share more, to let myself out into the world. And that has undoubtedly been good for me; for my confidence, for my anxious side, for my understanding of myself and the world and, yes, for my business.

Which brings me back to an old favourite: the fount of wisdom that is Steven Pressfield's *The War of Art*. Pressfield says, 'The more important a call or action is to our soul's evolution, the more Resistance we will feel toward pursuing it.' Those difficult times, the pain and fear that wraps us up sometimes, can be a compass to what matters. We can step into that pain and fear knowing that it will evolve us. That doesn't make those days good, but it's something, at least.

And this, I suspect, is the answer for those like Millman and for those of us who don't have *that* kind of success-drive but still keep stretching ourselves, keep asking 'what next?' We are driven to develop and grow and learn by evolution. And for the good of us, and our souls, we should take the next step. And then the next one. And the next.

# Chapter Thirty-One

# It's the Small Things That Will Change Your Life and It Doesn't Matter Which Ones

*Written on 21st December, 2018*

It's that time of year again. People are sharing so many end-of-year reviews, full of the amazing things they have done. Tips for what will help you transform your life in 2019. And by the middle of January, there will be even more.

I felt annoyed this morning. I thought about humans and how we like stories, and how we love the idea of stories like David and Goliath: the skilful/lucky moment (of genius) that allows someone who shouldn't be able to do something to succeed extraordinarily. How we love *that* part of the story. We love it, I think, because it implies there's a shortcut. A magic thing, that if we can just work out what it is will make everything different.

But if there's anything I've learned from three and a half years of spending hundreds of hours supporting people to create change in their lives (and thousands of hours more thinking and learning about how to do that) it's this: that's not how it works! How it works is this:

*Make a commitment to making a small change every day. AND STICK TO IT.*

That's it. That's all you need to do. We love the idea of learning from someone else. From how someone amazing – whether it's Steve Jobs or Tim Ferriss or Usain Bolt or Michelle Obama – has done things; how they have changed their lives. And there are wonderful things to learn from all of them. But what matters is finding the small thing that *you* can commit to every day. That's what will make a massive difference to the normal life of a normal person. Whether you're Steve, Tim, Usain, Michelle, me or you. Small changes.

By all means learn from these people and all the amazing people out there telling great stories. There have never been more stories to read or listen to, and some of them are wonderfully told. But don't imagine that any of the wonderful stories happen in any way other than someone doing something small on a regular basis. Even if some don't happen like that, it is *far better* to believe that they all do. So, choose to believe it.

Use the stories you hear to find the one small thing that you can do every day or every week, which over time will add up into what you want. The possibilities are endless, and the suggestions are too. One of my clients told me with fury how frustrating it was that everyone was telling her about 'exactly what to do' to build her business. It's impossible. We freeze when it's like that. And the truth is, *it doesn't matter which she chooses*. She just needs to choose one and commit to it and keep doing it.

Did you get that?

*It doesn't matter which way to change your life you choose. You just need to choose one.*

I had a client whose life was transformed in a week by creating a morning practice. It came from nowhere in one of our conversations as he told a story about a friend who was doing a PhD in happiness. One of the things that makes you happier, according to his friend, is writing down five things you're grateful for every day. My client did that, for a week, over his morning cup of tea, and came back looking and feeling and speaking completely differently. I'd never seen anything like it.

I received some amazing coaching from my friend Phil Bolton earlier in the year (after the experience with the client above, so I really should have known better) and out of it came a commitment for me to ask myself, every work day:

*What is in best service of my goals today?*

The focus of that question every day – and it takes me two minutes or so – has made me more productive, more focused and more fulfilled. I know where to put my energy and when I look back on the previous day I know what I have and haven't done. And I know a little more of why. I don't manage it every day, of course; I miss it sometimes, because I'm human. I missed it yesterday. But that doesn't stop me. I just recommit.

Clinical Psychologist Jordan Peterson talks about comparison. It's hard in this day and age (so hard!) not to compare ourselves to other people. He gives us another choice: compare yourself to you of yesterday, not someone else of today. He offers a different question to ask, every day: 'What could I do, that I would [choose to] do, to make life a little better?' You could change it, if you want, to something different. Perhaps, 'What could I do, that I would choose to do, to make the world a little bit better?' Then do it.

Working with a client, I worked out that if we make a one per cent improvement to our life every day for a year, our life will be 37 times better by the end. That's the maths. And one per cent doesn't feel like too much. Even if you only make a one per cent change once a week, your life will be almost twice as good by the end of the year. Wow! Who wouldn't want that?

Last year, I wrote about a question I was going to ask this year, every week. I didn't manage it every week, but I did answer it a lot. It was, 'Which one thing that drains me of energy will I stop doing this week?' That question has led to big things like me worrying less and massively improving my financial planning. It has also led to smaller but no less significant things, like choosing to consume alcohol and sugar differently, stopping playing on the computer or social media sooner than I otherwise would have. These may look smaller, but they are massively impactful for me as I try to feel better more, and as I negotiate the more addiction-prone parts of my personality.

I'm aware of the irony of giving these examples when I started this article feeling frustrated by all the stories out there, but the message I want to give you is this:

IT DOESN'T MATTER WHAT YOU CHOOSE.

You just have to choose some way of making your life a tiny bit better, every day or every week or every month. The smaller the better; make it something you can do even on a day when everything is closing in. Even on the days when things are really hard. And then make yourself do it. And recommit when you slip.

It's not easy. It's really hard, especially for some people. But it's magical and heroic. More magical and heroic than luckily hitting a giant with a stone by chance. Because it's what ordinary people do. It's hard. It's a struggle. It's what *anyone* can do. And it can change your life.

# Chapter Thirty-Two
# Dance the Dance With Uncertainty Again

*Written on 10th January, 2018*

The dance we each do with uncertainty is the scourge of creativity, of adventure, and of living the unlived lives within us.

It holds us back.

It holds us up.

It holds us in.

It goes something like this:

Something is happening with an uncertain outcome. Maybe it's a job move or deciding whether to share your writing with your friends or family. Perhaps it's deciding whether to travel to a country you haven't been to before. Perhaps it's deciding whether to go on the same holiday you've been on for the past five years or choose something new.

And underneath, that is where it almost always hits us: do I do what I've always done, or do I do something new?

Now there's no problem doing what we've always done. It's what makes the world go around. Imagine if you tried to travel to work a new way *every day*. In the end it would take hours, cost hundreds of pounds and... well... be a bit pointless.

But if you don't do something new simply because of uncertainty, that's different. Take a moment. Pause. Check that.

Because uncertainty is scary. Because of our wiring – whether originating in evolution or fearful education systems or concerned parents – uncertainty almost always comes from *it might not work*.

It might not work. It might go wrong. And if it doesn't work, if it goes wrong then... disaster. Embarrassment, loneliness, abandonment, death. (Or at least that's the pattern that my thoughts mostly follow, if I really dig in).

So, remember, we are brave people. I am brave. You are brave. Sometimes, we face uncertainty. We look 'it might not work' in the eye and we do it anyway. Because we're brave. Because we're bloody minded. Because 'it might work'.

And then? Is it over?

Well, some of it is over. Confidence is a result of our experience. Once we have left one job it's easier to leave the next. Once we have posted one article it's easier to post the next.

But it's not all over. Because there's still uncertainty next time. If we're lucky, maybe we transcend and include the old uncertainty. We truly learn that if someone doesn't like our writing, we won't end up in abandonment and death. And we learn that if someone does like our writing, we actually move further away from abandonment and death (this is me again). Then it's only new uncertainty that is there to hold us back. If we're unlucky, then we don't transcend and include it this time. And it seems that the next article, the next date, the next decision is as wrapped in uncertainty as this one. And so, we dance the dance again.

But I want to tell you that no matter how you feel, it's *never* the same dance. You are always carrying with you the experience of your success and your failure. If you are paying attention then you are always more certain next time, even on those rare occasions when you are only more certain of the uncertainty. So, what I am asking of you, what we are all asking of you, is to dance again.

Be brave. Be bloody-minded. Believe: it might work. And dance the dance again.

# Afterword

*Written on 28th February, 2022*

Sitting down to write the afterword of this book feels strange. Even with the timer. I feel a little tingle of tears in my eyes. Because I don't know if this book has been enough. And the truth is, no book can be. No book can give you the courage and bloody-mindedness, the skill and agility, the belief and trust to keep going, especially when things are tough.

You already have that. You have it inside you. And all I can really hope for is to be some small catalyst for those things, to release them that little bit more. To tell you what 12-minutes a week, every week, for years, might create. And to show you what it has created, this book and the others in the series. And to tell you how it has changed me, completely. And how different my life is as someone who can make a promise and keep a habit over years.

Not just any habit, either. A habit of creativity, a habit of courage, a habit of growth. That's why things have changed for me really – each article has grown me, my creativity, my courage. So that now I know things about myself that I couldn't have known if I had given up.

It almost doesn't matter what habit you choose, as I wrote in the penultimate chapter. Any habit, sustained over years, will make you into someone who can make a commitment to themselves and keep it. And that will create possibility.

But if you make your habit, your 12- or 20- or 60- or 213- or 1-Minute Method, something more than that, then even more can change. If it is connected to the work that is calling you – the thing that unique, wonderful, scrumpled, messy, glorious you are here to create. If it is connected to that, then something even more amazing might happen.

Time will have been on your side over the days, weeks, months, even years of the habit. And you might wake up, like I did, having almost by accident (but not by accident) created something. You won't know for sure what it is at the start, and trying to know will stop you; will distract you; will make you give up. And at the end you will be surprised. Surprised what a little guts, a little stubbornness, a little unwillingness to quit can get you.

Most people quit. That's the truth. That's why the tortoises win. The people who, like me, keep making something week after week. That's why I've written more than some of my friends and colleagues even though they started writing before me. They took breaks. I didn't.

I didn't know that was a quality I had. But I started making and I didn't stop. I didn't quit. I didn't give up. And hundreds of articles later, things are different.

That's what I want for you. But not just for you. Like I said at the start of this book, this is about more than just you.

Work that matters takes time. It takes time to master a craft, to practise until you become something more, something unusual, in any field. And if we want to change the world, we are going to need people who are willing to not quit in the face of challenges, in the face of criticism, in the face of inertia.

We need people who are willing to show up again and again and again and again.

And again.

I hope you'll be one of those people.

Start small. 12 minutes is enough. And obsess about 'enough' not about 'as much as possible'. 12 minutes is enough. Start there.

Just 12 minutes. Once a week. For three years. And anything can happen.

Because it isn't just 12 minutes, at least not in my experience. Those 12 minutes of persistence, courage and creativity will ripple out into your life, changing your relationships, your work, your mindset.

Persistence, courage and 12 minutes a week will take you a long way. Further than you can imagine.

But it might not be 12 minutes for you. I know that and you know that. One of the wonderful things about choosing 12 minutes for my writing practice is that it's incredibly arbitrary. Most trains from Clapham Junction to Waterloo don't even take 12 minutes. They take 7 or 13. 12 minutes is just a symbol.

It's a symbol to remind me and to remind you to not

give up. To keep practising, day after day, week after week, month after month, year after year. Maybe, although I don't know yet, decade after decade.

Keep practising, keep creating.

Keep making the world better, one step at a time.

Don't give up.

# Help Spread the Word

I believe that the world is a better place when people are creating things; when people move out of the hell of procrastination and make things that make a difference.

If you agree with me, or if this book has helped you, please help someone else to keep going when they want to give up by doing one of two things:

## 1. Review this book on Amazon

It really can't be overstated how important reviews are to help a book reach the people it's intended to help. If you have taken something positive from reading this book, please spare five minutes of your time to help someone else find their something positive too. You never know where it might take them.

Even just a few words will make a big difference.

## 2. Tell someone about this book

Do you know someone who always talks about the book they'll write or the business they'll start or the creative project they've just thought of? Maybe they never start. Or maybe they start but they give up, even though you know and they know that they don't want to, deep down.

If you do, tell them about this book. Tell them the story of how I wrote it. Give it to them for their birthday or for Christmas. It might be exactly what they need.

# Please Share Your Work: Free E-book

If you want to make a difference you have to *start* and you have to *keep going*.

And if you want to make a difference, at some point your work has to connect with someone else. I want your work to make a difference and that's why I'm giving you a draft copy of the fourth book in the 12-Minute Method series *for free*.

To get your copy visit

**www.robbieswale.com/12minute-method-downloads**

or scan this QR code:

This book, provisionally titled *How to Share Your Work Even When You're Scared*, contains more practical inspiration aimed at getting your idea out into the world.

The full book will be published in late 2022, but this draft version will always be free to you via the above link.

# Stay Up to Date About The 12-Minute Method

This is the second in a series of books created to support you through the creative process. The next two books in the series will be published later in 2022.

To be the first to hear about those books, other 12-Minute Method developments, and my other work, sign up to my mailing list at:

**www.robbieswale.com/mailing-list**

# Acknowledgments

*Written on 28th January, 2022*

In *How to Start When You're Stuck*, I wrote that I thought every author should write their acknowledgments in a 12-minute sitting, to have an excuse for inevitably forgetting someone. But, it turned out, that wasn't a good idea, because I did forget someone and that didn't feel better because I had a 12-minute excuse.

The person I forgot was Joni Zwart. Joni gave me time, encouragement and the expertise and experience developed in a career in publishing (before she moved on to other exciting things – read more at **www.jonizwart.nl**) to help me navigate the publishing industry and understand what *I* wanted for this book, the others in the series and the other book I'm working on. She was generous, insightful, encouraging and willing to say things that were probably a bit difficult to say (and difficult for me to hear) especially between friends.

Without her contribution, this book wouldn't have made its way to you in this form, a form that in this moment feels like exactly the right way for it to have made its way to you. Thanks, Joni, and sorry I forgot you last time.

Thanks, of course, to all the people who have practically worked on this book: Steve Creek, Tim Pettingale, Joseph Alexander (and their team at **www.self-published.co.uk**).

Thanks to the coaches that have supported me: Joel, who helped me start, of course deserves the special mention. But also, the coaches and mentors that supported me as I kept going with this practice, with my business, with my relationship, with all the things that required everything in this book and more to not give up on. In particular, Mike Toller, Rich Litvin, Katie Harvey, Robert Holden – thank you.

Thank you to the people who wrote words to be included in the 'impact' section of this book and the last one: Nadine, Karena, Paul, Peter, Jo, Hannah, Michelle, Emma, David, Bryon, Robert, Alex – thank you. Reading what you wrote has been one of the ways I have kept going through the publishing process. It turns out that even writing a series of books about the creative process doesn't get you out of the struggles. But it does help. In particular, what helps is having 12 people who you respect and admire writing things about your work. On the dark days, when resistance rears its head the most, remembering that each of you wrote those things kept me going and helped me deal with myself. 'They are people of integrity. They wouldn't have written that if it wasn't true,' I told myself. And it really, really helped.

Thanks to my family and friends: my mum, dad, brother and sister. My oldest friends. My newer friends and colleagues. Those relationships that sustain me in the dark days. You know who you are, and I hope you know how much you mean to me.

Thank you to Emma. Who supports me through all the times I struggle to deal with myself, through all the dark days. And who makes every day at least a little less dark. And to Leah, that little ball of 13-month-old colour and aliveness who has taught me new things about patience, persistence and what matters in the world.

Thank you to all the people who taught me about the sheer beauty of persistence, of showing up. The clients of great courage, the artists who shared their vulnerability and struggles.

Thank you to everyone who bought my first book – it has been genuinely surprising to me that you did. I know, given everything, it perhaps shouldn't be, but it is. And one of the absolutely most pleasurable things has been people sending me pictures of themselves with the book, or holding it up in a video call, in different parts of the country and the world. And people telling me about how they shared it with their loved ones, who they thought might need it.

And lastly, thank you to you. Thanks for showing up. For reading this. And for doing the work, whatever work it is. For keeping going even when the inertia of the world tries to stop you. It's easier to give up, in so many ways. Thank you for not doing that.

The work you are doing matters. At least, it does to you, and it does to me. And if you keep going, and you share it, I think it'll matter to someone else, too.

# How I Wrote a Book in 12 Minutes: Notes About the Process

For those who are interested, I wanted to add a few words about how this book was created, and the idea of creating a book in 12 minutes, to supplement what I described in the introduction and throughout the book. I share this to give those among you who want to do something similar the power to choose how you do that.

I imagined originally that this series would simply be a compilation of the pieces as they were posted online, but once something starts to become a book (or a series of books), some extra decisions need to be made.

First, it felt important to give myself a little more leeway than I do with the articles when they first go online. I gave myself an extra proofread/edit of the whole book, then I sent it to my friend, Steve Creek, a professional copy editor, to give it a once over.

The spirit of those edits was to improve it, so it could support people even more. It was to tighten and clarify. The substance of the articles was not changed significantly – a sentence was added or removed here and there, a few titles made more relevant or punchier. There were a few tweaks to make the language and sense clearer, or to fix bits that were hazy on detail because the original was written in 12 minutes and there wasn't time to look up precisely what someone had said. After the book came back from Steve, there was some broader feedback and some rearranging of the pieces, then it sat, pretty much untouched, for about two years (more on that another time).

When I came back to it, with the help of Tim Pettingale and Joseph Alexander from **www.self-published.co.uk**, we realised it would work even better as a series, but that required another edit from me, again leaving the substance but tightening and making clearer a sentence here and there, or adding a few words or a couple of sentences to make it clear why a particular piece belonged here, in this part of the book or series. As the publishing process went on, the book received an edit from Tim and another two reads and light edits from me. I noticed, as each time passed, that I was more willing to tweak for clarity and impact and to more firmly place a piece where it sat in the book. But, as you can tell from reading, these pieces are absolutely imperfect, and many are pretty much exactly as they were originally written on the train or with the 12-minute timer.

At different stages, I also added in introductions to each part, to help tie the book together. Those introductions, the notes and pages about free gifts, and this piece are the only bits not originally written in 12 minutes, although even with the introductions, which mostly didn't take 12 minutes, I set the timer to make sure I got out of my own way and got going. That's how I work. The 12-Minute Method section at the start was written in the same spirit, but I had to reset the timer three times to have time to say everything that needed saying (The 36-Minute Method!).

A few pieces from the series of articles didn't quite belong in a series about creating what you are called to create, so those were removed. Remarkably few pieces from the first three years of the writing practice overlapped in content enough that a piece needed to be removed, but there were a couple, so they came out. I felt that a few more didn't help the flow of the books, so they came out too. This process was surprisingly hard, but it served the books to remove them. All these pieces can be read on LinkedIn where they were originally posted, on my website, or in The Cutting Room, a short ebook available at:

**www.robbieswale.com/12minute-method-downloads**

I wasn't sure where to draw the line with which set of 12-minute articles would make up the series, but on my deadline to send the book to Steve, I realised it was three years and one day since I started the weekly practice (after the initial five pieces). So, what makes up this book and the other three in the series are the five original parts of The Train Series and almost exactly three years of weekly articles.

And that, pretty much, is how you write a book (or four!) in 12 minutes.